CULTURAL KNOWLEDGE
IN ORGANIZATIONS

To the Culture Club
and those
whom I love most

CULTURAL KNOWLEDGE IN ORGANIZATIONS
Exploring the Collective Mind

Sonja A. Sackmann

SAGE PUBLICATIONS
The International Professional Publishers
Newbury Park   London   New Delhi

For information address:

SAGE Publications, Inc.
2455 Teller Road
Newbury Park, California 91320

SAGE Publications Ltd.
6 Bonhill Street
London EC2A 4PU
United Kingdom

SAGE Publications India Pvt. Ltd.
M-32 Market
Greater Kailash I
New Delhi 110 048 India

Printed in the United States of America

Library of Congress Cataloging-in-Publication Data

Sackmann, Sonja, 1955-
   Cultural knowledge in organizations : exploring the collective
mind / Sonja A. Sackmann.
     p.   cm.
   Includes bibliographical references and index.
   ISBN 0-8039-4292-3. — ISBN 0-8039-4293-1 (pbk.)
   1. Corporate culture. I. Title
HD58.7.S23 1991
302.3'5—dc20   91-14913
                                                        CIP

92 93 94 15 14 13 12 11 10 9 8 7 6 5 4 3 2

Sage Production Editor: Astrid Virding

Contents

Acknowledgments

A large number of people have contributed to this work at various stages and in various ways—directly and indirectly, on theoretical, practical, or emotional grounds, as advisers, colleagues, students, and as dear friends, both in the United States and in Europe. I am grateful to all of them.

Nevertheless there are a few people I would like to acknowledge individually. Special thanks are due to those who have directly contributed to the research: Theodore Williams, president of BIND, who gave me his trust in allowing me to study the company and the freedom to do whatever I felt was necessary for my study; Garry Linden and Marc Labe, general managers of the PC and the GA divisions, allowed me to interview their employees despite their heavy work load; and all the people at BIND who gave me their time and trust and who shared with me their information and knowledge about BIND's innovation and changes.

Harry Briggs from Sage encouraged me to continue polishing this manuscript before moving on to the next project.

Several people have been intellectually stimulating and have contributed with a range of perspectives they brought to my attention. Rodolfo Alvarez helped me strengthen my methodology through our critical and stimulating discussions. Eric

Flamholtz helped me sharpen my perspective and my arguments with his critical view toward my theoretical framework. Lynne Zucker supported my way of approaching the concept of culture applied to organizations on both theoretical and methodological levels. Fred Massarik supported and nourished my interests in phenomenologically oriented research and convinced me in our talks in Frankfurt, Los Angeles, and New York to join UCLA's Graduate School of Management. Craig Lundberg's suggestions were very helpful in producing a more readable manuscript. Peter Dachler and Jürg Manella, who share with me an interest in social constructivism, have been supportive of its implementation both in my teaching and in my consulting.

This work is hard to imagine without the weekly meetings of the "culture club." I am deeply grateful to my two comembers and French Roast drinkers Maggi Phillips and Dick Goodman. Through Maggi's interest in the subject I could sustain mine; I could bounce off my ideas and learn from hers. Her critiques helped me express myself more clearly and her emotional Jamaican-Aries-biased support helped me wade through the "muddiest" and darkest sides of the research process and its writings. Dick Goodman took time to discuss my ideas, no matter how well thought through they were. He listened patiently and critically to all kinds of concerns and allowed me to let off steam that had accumulated during my thought processes and my research.

I am truly grateful to my family for their emotional support, which could always bridge the long distances between the Black Forest and my different locations—Heidelberg, New York, Los Angeles, or now St. Gallen. Even though I did not follow the path that my parents had intended for me, they accepted my stubbornness and are proud of me and my work. And finally, Wolfi, thanks for your technical help with the manuscript and for your endless patience and emotional support when I was sitting at my computer on beautiful weekends.

ONE

Introduction

The topic of culture has entered the business world. This does not necessarily imply that the level of cultivation has increased in corporate life, that business manners are more polished nowadays, that managers show more taste in the way they dress or in their choice of food and drinks, or that sophisticated artwork can be admired on the walls of corporations. Instead, when the term is used by managers and organizational researchers, they link it with the success or failure of a firm.

A growing number of publications suggest that corporate culture influences an organization's performance[1]. Consequently executives and managers want to know how to manage corporate culture—how to influence or change it to obtain the best culture possible for achieving excellence in performance. As a result the list of "how-to's" has increased at a fast rate. Offerings include culture audits, a matching of corporate culture with a firm's strategy, or recommendations about how to manage and change a firm's culture.

A critical review of the literature reveals, however, that empirically based knowledge about culture in organizational settings is rather scarce and spotty. While some people offer and sell prescriptions to practitioners, others are still exploring the meaning and implications of culture in its organizational setting. The frequent use of the same term hides differences in meanings and assumptions. And the widespread interest in the topic does not help because there are almost as many definitions and understandings of *culture* as people writing about it. When organizational researchers or practitioners talk about culture in organizations, they may not mean the same thing.

To some extent these differences have been imported with the topic from its anthropological base in which a century of investigation has not led to a common understanding. Furthermore most anthropological concepts of culture have emerged in studies of rather isolated societies. It is, therefore, questionable whether these concepts and their associated assumptions can be directly applied to organizations. Today's firms cannot afford to be isolated and homogeneous if they want to survive. In addition societies and organizations differ in several respects. Organizations are an element of society. They tend to be smaller, to be shorter lived, and to have a more immediate intention. This implies that the differences in context and resulting implications between former tribes and today's organizations need first to be examined critically before one can make prescriptions about culture in organizations.

Matters are further complicated by the different interests in the topic that are, to some extent, due to different professional training and adherence to different cultural paradigms. While some organizational researchers pursue the same interest as their anthropological colleagues in trying to gain a better understanding of cultural settings, the functional aspects of culture seem to attract most attention among practitioners. How can a firm's culture be shaped for the best results? Within this perspective *culture* is transformed into a technical term or a variable that can be brought under managerial control. Culture is assumed to act as a control mechanism, to create organizational commitment, to achieve integration within a firm, or to help it adapt to external changes. And certain kinds of culture promise to produce a better performance than others.

Little research has, however, been conducted to examine these assumed functional aspects of culture or other aspects of its nature in organizational settings. The few empirical studies are more "spotlike" and reflect the different interests and training of the researchers. Topics of research interests range from corporate culture as such to unique views of professionals in organizations. They include the study of stories, scripts, legends, humor, the founder's influence on culture, the influence of belief systems on decision making, or the effectiveness of certain cultures.[2]

An evaluation of the existing literature leads to the conclusion that most academicians and practitioners agree on the importance of culture applied to organizations but that major questions remain unanswered. What does culture mean in an organizational context? Is it the same concept as used in anthropology, in sociology, or in everyday life? Of what does it consist? What are its characteristics? Where is it located and how can it be understood?

If culture is to survive its fashionable wave and turn into a useful and meaningful concept both for organizational researchers and for practitioners, it is necessary to spend more effort on empirical research rather than on debating opinions. This book will present the origins, process, and results of a study that I designed to shed light on some of these fundamental questions.

ORGANIZATION OF THE BOOK

This book is organized into 12 chapters and three appendixes. Chapter 2 discusses different perspectives of culture both in the social sciences and in the managerial and organizational literature. The reader will realize that the managerial literature draws predominantly and quite selectively from some of the concept's anthropological roots. In the organizational and managerial literature, I differentiate and discuss three major perspectives with their strengths and limitations; a holistic, a variable, and a cognitive perspective.

Three major problems arise from a critical evaluation of these conceptions of culture. These problems refer to the components of culture, to its dimensions, and to assumptions about culture in organizational settings. They have led to an alternative view of culture in organizational settings that is presented in Chapter 3. This view is based on collective sense-making mechanisms, or cognitions. I differentiate four different kinds of cultural knowledge that refer to descriptions, cause-and-effect relationships, prescriptions, and underlying assumptions. Together they form a cultural knowledge map.

I applied this framework of cultural knowledge in a study to investigate its usefulness and comprehensiveness in terms of understanding the essence of a specific cultural setting. I also wanted to know more about its dynamics, that is, how cultural knowledge is created and perpetuated. Furthermore I addressed the nature of culture in terms of the formation and location of potential cultural subgroups.

A special methodology was designed for this study that allowed me to surface cultural cognitions from the insider's perspective and to test an emerging hypotheses in regard to the formation of cultural groupings. Its most important features are described at the end of Chapter 3 so that the reader who is not interested in methodological issues has a general idea how I obtained the results that are discussed in Chapters 4 to 8. Those who are interested in the details of the study may read Appendix A: Methodology. This appendix discusses methodological problems associated with the study of culture and describes the specific research methodology. Topics include the research design, the research sites, the methods of data collection, and data analysis and interpretation.

Chapter 4 summarizes the major findings of the study to provide the reader with a framework for pursuing the more detailed descriptions and discussions of the research findings in Chapters 5 to 8. The findings relate to the nature of culture in organizational settings and reveal that its structure is more complex than previously assumed. The proposed framework of cultural knowledge was further specified. Both the developed methodology and the proposed framework of cultural knowledge turned out to be useful in understanding one firm's cultural setting.

Chapters 5 to 8 describe and discuss the various findings in detail. Chapter 5 addresses the findings in regard to the descriptive kind of cultural knowledge (dictionary knowledge), which includes the content and structure of four major themes and cultural groupings. The themes refer to the firm's goal and accomplishments and its strategy, structure, and organizational members. Seven cultural groupings emerged according to a special grouping mechanism that is discussed in detail.

Chapter 6 addresses insights regarding the causal-analytical kind of knowledge (directory knowledge). Four major themes emerged that are all related to organizational processes. They address the way tasks are accomplished, how people relate to each other, how the firm collectively adapts and changes, and how it acquires and perpetuates knowledge. These four processes occurred in similar ways across the studied divisions and cultural groupings. I discuss this phenomenon as cultural synergism.

The findings about the prescriptive kind of knowledge (recipe knowledge) are examined in Chapter 7. Chapter 8 explores the findings regarding axiomatic knowledge. Several axioms or basic assumptions surfaced that have influenced the formation and processes of institutionalizing this knowledge.

Chapter 9 proposes a general framework of cultural knowledge called cultural knowledge map. Relevant content areas are integrated with the four kinds of cultural knowledge into the cultural knowledge map.

Chapter 10 examines the relationships that surfaced among cultural knowledge, strategy, and organizational processes. More specifically I consider cultural knowledge as a link between strategic issues and organizational processes.

Chapter 11 summarizes the study and draws conclusions on the nature and concept of culture in organizational settings.

Chapter 12 outlines the study's implications for future research and for understanding cultural settings. Specific questions for future research are listed in Appendix B.

The reader who is interested in the research process from an existential point of view should refer to Appendix C: Epilogue. It contains those aspects of the research process that are usually not included in a technical report, such as dealing with a research topic and searching for, entering, and being present in the research site as well as reflections of the researcher in action.

NOTES

1. Some of the frequently cited authors who suggest such a performance impact of culture are, for example, Baker (1980), Peters and Waterman (1982), Deal and Kennedy (1982), or an article in *Business Week* ("Corporate Culture," 1980).

2. Stories, scripts, and legends were, for example, studied by Wilkins (1978), Wilkins and Martin (1979), and Martin (1982). Schein (1983) investigated the founder's influence on culture. Humor was studied by Vinton (1983). Sapienza (1985), in her study, addressed the influence of top managements' belief systems on decision making, while Denison (1984) and Barney (1986) examined the effectiveness of certain cultures and their impact on performance.

Existing Perspectives on Culture

The original and central domain of the concept of culture is anthropology. Since the end of the eighteenth century, anthropologists have been investigating culture as their basic and central concept. Malinowski and Chase[1] have gone so far as suggesting that it is the foundation stone and the most central problem of all social science. Anthropologists have, therefore, exerted a large influence on the concept's meanings. But culture has also received attention in the disciplines of sociology and social psychology before it was "discovered" in the fields of management and organizational theory, where Peters[2] considers it to be the "most important stuff around."

Although anthropologists, sociologists, organizational theorists, and managers use the same term and similar definitions, the meanings that they associate with *culture* are not always the same. This is due to the different contexts and respectively different assumptions associated with these contexts. They are related to differing interests regarding culture and lead to different expectations about what the concept can accomplish. Hence different lenses have been used to explore the theoretical base of culture, to explain its impact, to study it, and to apply it to organizations.

An introduction to some of the heritage of the culture concept will help to better understand the conceptual diversity or confusion in the managerial and organizational literature.

HERITAGE OF THE "CULTURE" CONCEPT

Langness[3] suggests that John Locke's "Essay on Human Understanding" set the metaphysical foundations for the concept dating back to 1690. While German sociologists explored the concept in the late eighteenth century in terms of civilization and cultivation of mankind,[4] Edward B. Tylor, one of the first anthropologists, introduced it into the English language only a century ago. In 1871 he defined *culture* as "that complex whole which includes knowledge, beliefs, art, morals, law, custom and any other capabilities and habits acquired by man as a member of society."[5]

Since that time anthropologists have set out to investigate culture. Their major—and common—interest was and still is to gain an understanding of human affairs. But, despite a century of exploration, it is impossible to find consensus among anthropologists on what culture is, what it means, what its characteristics are, what it is composed of, what it does, or how it should be studied. Kroeber and Kluckhohn[6] list, for example, more than 250 different definitions. These definitions include components such as ideas, concepts, ideologies, values, attitudes, goals, norms, learned behaviors, symbols, rites, rituals, customs, myths, habits, or artifacts such as tools and other material representations. Behind this diversity of concepts and their selective use stand different assumptions about what culture is or what its most important components are. These assumptions have led to different foci in anthropologists' studies and ultimately to different conceptions of culture.[7]

In anthropology the term *culture* generally has been used to designate two different things. One refers to Tylor's complex whole comprising everything that is considered cultural. A tribe or a social group is studied as a culture that may produce and have cultural artifacts. The second use of the term *culture* refers to specific aspects that are considered components of culture such as artifacts, rituals, customs, knowledge, ideas, or symbols.

The concept's connotative meaning depends on the anthropological school that is—or was—influenced by its main representatives' assumptions about the topic, their main foci and interests in research as well as the special zeitgeist. Five major approaches to culture can be distinguished. Each one is, to some extent, a reaction to the preceding approach.[8] These approaches or schools of thought are listed in Table 2.1, including their main representatives, their access to culture, their predominant interest in its study, and their underlying assumptions and/or assertions.

Early conceptions of culture in anthropology were influenced by an evolutionary perspective that implied different degrees of progress and cultivation between cultured and primitive societies. The boundaries of culture were seen as being identical to societal boundaries. Culture was conceptualized as a complex whole that includes cognitive, behavioral, and material aspects. Its main representatives, such as Edward Tylor,[9] were interested in discovering the grand laws of evolution and origins, and they assumed that educated people were superior to so-called primitive people, who had fallen from grace.

This early evolutionary view of culture has been replaced today by a synthetic perspective that incorporates the more useful aspects of the theory of evolution.[10] But the early perspective can still be found in everyday language to refer to acquired habits of dressing, eating, or knowledge within humanistic areas. This special use and meaning of the term *culture* refers to the concept of cultivation—the process of consciously improving human conditions. If this meaning is implied, *cultivation* is the more appropriate term to use.

Historical Particularism was a reaction to the early evolutionary perspective. Franz Boas,[11] the main representative of this approach, emphasized the historical nature of culture and its artifacts, traits, and elements. He considered culture particularistic with no unifying thread among its components.

Table 2.1 The Major Anthropological Aproaches: Main Representatives, Foci and Interests of Study, Assumptions

Anthropological Approach	Main Focus of Study	Main Representatives	Major Interests in Research	Assumptions/Assertions
Cultural Evolution	Culture = complex whole, which includes cognitive, behavioral, and material aspects acquired by human beings	C. Taylor (1871, 1903)	Search for grand laws for evolution and origins	Educated are superior to "primitive" people, who have fallen from grace
Historical Particularism	Physical anthropology facts, traits, and elements	F. Boas (1896, 1940)	Collect data in situ and discover their sui generis principles	Anthropology should be historical, inductive, and scientific The individual is an important unit of study
	"Supraorganic" (the nonindividual)	A. L. Kroeber (1917)	Discover patterns and configurations of culture (search for a grand theory)	Anthropology = history (rather than science) Individuals are subordinate to culture
Functionalism	Discover the structure of a natural system and try to understand how each part functions in relation to the system	A. R. Radcliffe-Brown (1952, 1957)	Social structure = abstraction from behavior (no interest in psychological or biological aspects)	Culture concept is less meaningful than the concept of social systems

(continued)

		Culture = set of rules for fitting people together into a system	Study of social structure: determine the function of behavior in terms of how well it serves the well-being of a group	Anthropology = science People are organized in systems that constitute wholes whose parts contribute to their wholeness
	B. Malinowski (1939, 1944)		How do the various elements of culture contribute to the whole?	Culture = an instrument through which human need are met (seven basic needs)
			Interested in psychological, biological, and social needs	
Cultural Materialism	J. Stuart (1955)	Culture = observable behavior	Environmental and technoenvironmental influences	Anthropology = science
	L. White (1959)	"Culturology" (culture exists independent of human beings) Culture = continuum of interacting elements even though individuals are carriers of cultural tradition	Science of culture	Ecology is determining influence on culture and its evolution
	M. Harris (1964)	Culture = behavior	Collective behaviors	Culture = behavior that is determined by techno-environmental factors

Table 2.1 Continued

Anthropological Approach	Main Focus of Study	Main Representatives	Major Interests in Research	Assumptions/Assertions
Cultural Idealism:				
psychological anthropology	Culture = integrated whole with consistency	R. Benedict (1934; 1942)	Culture is a determinant of personality	Culture = consistent pattern of thought and action = integrated whole
		M. Mead (1939)	(= different styles of life)	Culture = personality of its members *and* determines personality of its members
	"Superorganic"	A. L. Kroeber (1917)		
	Culture = something internalized by human beings as a world of meaning	E. Sapir (1917)		The language a person internalizes affects the way he or she perceives the world
ethnography	Cultural descriptions based on language	J. P. Spradley (1972) H. Garfinkel (1967)	Use of ethnoscience to study the insiders' view	History is alive in people's recollections
structuralism	Collective unconscious	C. Lévi-Strauss (1920; 1949)	Psycological aspects of structure fundamental structures of the mind	
symbolic anthropology	Culture = primarily a system of symbols	C. Geertz (1973) V. Turner (1967)	Combination of emic and etic descriptions	Symbols are involved in social processes, they become associated with human interests, purposes, ends and means

Understanding culture implied detailed observations and recordings of customs in their context to uncover their "sui generis" principles. This particularistic view of culture with a focus on the study of material artifacts in situ was overcome by some of Boas's students.

Kroeber and Benedict,[12] for example, made major efforts to unravel configurations and patterns among observed behaviors and artifacts. To make institutions intelligible, their sui generis principles had to be discovered *including* their configurations and patterns. These were seen as a finite set of components selected from a range of possibilities. They considered the sui generis principles congruent with each other, constituting a configuration that forms an integrated and consistent whole. This whole represents the unique property of one peculiar culture. One of the major differences between the two anthropologists, however, was that Kroeber focused on the "superorganic"—those aspects that are beyond the individual level—in his search for a grand theory. Benedict, on the contrary, emphasized psychological aspects.

The main representatives of Functionalism, such as Radcliffe-Brown and Malinowski, were predominantly interested in social structure. In their search for the structure or set of rules of a natural system, they investigated how each part functions in relation to the system. This function was then evaluated in terms of how well it served or promoted the well-being of a group. Both treat anthropology as a science as opposed to history. While Radcliffe-Brown saw the culture concept as less meaningful than the concept of social systems, Malinowski considered culture an instrument through which basic human needs are met.

Representatives of Cultural Materialism took an even more pragmatic approach to culture with their focus on observable behavior and "interesting elements" even though individuals were considered carriers of culture. Furthermore they considered culture determined by technoenvironmental factors. These were the focus of their scientific studies.

The representatives of Cultural Idealism take an opposed view. Even though they fall into four broad categories, all of them focus on cognitive aspects, that is, the invisible mental constructions that people have. The four different directions are psychological anthropology, structuralism, ethnography, and symbolic anthropology. Even though they represent distinctive approaches, they are complementary within the Cultural Idealism perspective.

Psychological anthropology included psychoanalytical considerations. On the one hand culture was seen to determine the personalities of its members, while on the other hand it represented the personality of its members. Sapir linked culture to the field of linguistics and saw it as something internalized by human beings as a world of meaning that affects the way they perceive the world.[13] Ethnography emerged with a focus on cultural descriptions based on language. In their studies ethnographers also attempt to understand a setting from the insiders' perspective—similar to Boas's *sui generis* principles.

Lévi-Strauss, the main representative of structuralism, focused on the collective unconscious and assumed that history is alive in people's recollections.[14] For symbolic anthropologists culture is primarily a system of symbols that are involved in social processes and that become associated with human interests, purposes, ends, and means. In their studies structuralists focus on both emic and etic perspectives, that is, the insiders' and the outsiders' views.

Despite these different schools of thought, the major interest of anthropologists has been in increasing understanding of the various facets of cultural phenomena. They search for the meaning underlying human creations, behaviors, and thoughts. They try to render "culture" intelligible by observing and interpreting observed cultural aspects. While research methods cover the range from historical to scientific approaches, including ethnographic and phenomenological ones, a large number of cultural anthropologists have used historical or ethnographic methods to trace, observe, and take account of events. They attempt to understand human actions in the contexts in which they occur. They attempt to reach beyond their initial role of an onlooker to finally understand the cultural setting from an insider's perspective and unravel the context's *sui generis* principles.

For their fieldwork cultural anthropologists have preferred to select small tribes or social groups to study the customs and artifacts of their members. The small-scale societies investigated have lived in rather secluded environments such as Africa, New Guinea, or certain islands.[15]

The major contribution of anthropology in developing the concept of culture lies, therefore, in detailed accounts of the cultural phenomena, such as rites, rituals, customs, habits, ceremonies, material artifacts, and patterns of thinking and behaving, of, however, rather esoteric, small-scale societies or tribes. The complexity of life is, however, far below that of today's major societies. Furthermore anthropologists have placed less importance on further abstraction from their descriptive data. Most of them were not interested in generalizing beyond the immediate context of their studies.

Both the focus on small-scale societies and the conceptualization of culture as a unique homogeneous configuration or pattern of a particular social group have perpetuated the idea of culture as a monolithic entity. Sociologists, who by tradition take a macro perspective in their study, have advocated a less homogeneous and monolithic view of culture. Sociological studies have explicitly focused on subgroups of society such as teenagers or cocktail waitresses. They have focused on groups in the urban community or on selected aspects of a social group such as the sense-making processes of judges.[16] In these endeavors, they have, however, not claimed to study *the* culture of, for example, the professional group "judges."

This more heterogeneous or pluralistic view of culture can also be found in the everyday uses of the term to refer to social movements such as *hippies, rockers, punks,* or *environmentalists.* In addition to pluralism, this usage of the term also implies that a person who belongs to one of these groups may also belong to another group. This group may have a social, ethnic, or racial basis such as parent, teenager, student; Catholic, Jewish, Mormon, or Protestant; Black, Caucasian, or Hispanic.

From this perspective culture is something much less unitary and unified. The sociologist Lipp even suggested that culture may be thought of as a loose association of ideas, as different themes, as different values, and as configurations of action.[17] This contrasts with the patterned view in which culture is conceptualized as an overarching integrative pattern that creates a condensed social reality.

This discussion about some of the heritage of culture, while less than comprehensive, supports the initial argument that social scientists are far from agreeing about the various facets of the phenomenon even though they use the same term. The fact that multitudes of meanings are attributed to culture and that multiple views of culture exist is characteristic not only of the social science literature but also of the managerial and organizational literature. This should not be surprising in light of the above review given that managerial or organizational authors draw predominantly—and selectively—from some of the concept's anthropological but rarely from its sociological roots.

While frequent uses of the same terms, definitions, and references have hidden the varying meanings in the literature of the early 1980s, scholars in the field have become increasingly aware of the complexity of culture when applied to organizations. It is a much more complicated endeavor than merely borrowing a few terms from a different discipline and applying them without detailed examination. I will discuss now the various applications and uses of *culture* in organizational settings.

CULTURE APPLIED TO ORGANIZATIONAL SETTINGS

Conceptions of culture in the organizational and managerial literature draw quite selectively from various anthropological and sociological sources. This selection tends to be based on the author's particular interest and approach. Some of the organizational scholars pursue the same interest as anthropologists. Through their work they try to gain an in-depth understanding of organizations as cultural settings. They are interested in human affairs within organizational boundaries. They treat culture as something that an organization *is* and hope to further develop existing theories of organizations through their insights. This stream of work represents, however, only one part.

The managerial work is predominantly guided by practitioners' interest in creating conditions for more effective organizations. The ultimate interest of managers in culture, therefore, goes beyond description, understanding, and explanation to prediction and control. As a result of this interest a variety of prescriptions about corporate or organizational culture have resulted in the literature. Understandings of the concept of culture focus predominantly on behavior and its functionality. Similar to anthropology the conceptions of organizational culture underlying cultural prescriptions tend to reveal more about the author than about the concept itself—even if the same terms are used. It seems fruitful at this point, therefore, to bracket the prescriptive interest in culture until more empirical data are available to guide prescriptive advice and actions.

From anthropology three conceptions of culture have had the most influence on the managerial literature: the pattern or configurationist view (Benedict, Kroeber, Kluckhohn), the manifestation-oriented view including Functionalism (Boas, White, Malinowski, Radcliffe-Brown), and an ideational or cognitive view including symbolism (Goodenough, Keesing, Geertz, Turner).[18] The latter one has been combined and elaborated with aspects of cognitive and learning psychology. Hence three broad perspectives of culture can be differentiated in the managerial literature that are relevant in this context, which are

(1) a *holistic* perspective,
(2) a *variable* perspective, and
(3) a *cognitive* perspective.

These three perspectives will now be described in detail. The boundaries between these three perspectives are not completely clear-cut. Overlaps exist, and one author may be found to apply different perspectives during her or his career depending on his or her particular focus in a specific paper or study. The three perspectives should be considered as three different emphases or orientations that are useful distinctions within this context.

The Holistic Perspective

The *holistic perspective* draws on the work of anthropologists such as Benedict, Kroeber, and Kluckhohn, who integrate cognitive, emotive, behavioral, and artifactual aspects of culture into one unified whole. Within this perspective *culture* is defined as patterned ways of thinking, feeling, and reacting that are acquired and transmitted mainly by symbols. They constitute the distinctive achievements of human groups, including their embodiments in artifacts. Culture has a core that consists of traditional—that is, historically derived—and selected ideas and their attached values. The resulting cultural system is, on the one hand, to be considered a product of action and, on the other, conditioning elements of further action.[19]

This holistic perspective of culture is widely accepted in the managerial literature. It represents an implicit reference point in thinking, writing, or talking about the elusive concept of culture in organizations. The following is an example of a typical definition of culture from this perspective (Tunstall, 1983, p. 5):

> Corporate culture may be described as a general constellation of beliefs, mores, customs, value systems, behavioral norms, and ways of doing business that are unique to each corporation, that set a pattern for corporate activities and actions, and that describe the implicit and emergent patterns of behavior and emotions characterizing life in the organization.

The holistic perspective captures well the multifaceted nature of culture. It can integrate its historical development with its dynamic evolutionary nature. However, this perspective does not lend itself easily to research. To study culture in organizations from this perspective implies a detailed long-term ethnography involving various sources of data and a focus on all possible aspects of culture, which result in rich setting-specific descriptions that make it difficult to distinguish conjecture from empirical evidence. Because ethnographies focus on the idiosyncratic aspects of a society's or a social group's culture, they cannot answer analytically oriented questions about the structural aspects of culture. Only a larger number of such studies could shed some light on general cultural aspects if their results are compiled and reanalyzed in retrospect from a higher level of analysis.

This has resulted in a somewhat schizophrenic situation. While many researchers define culture from this holistic perspective, they tend to focus their actual research on either the visible manifestations or the invisible culture core. Despite this apparently minimal difference, the two foci are usually accompanied by fundamentally different assumptions about culture. Those who focus on the visible and more tangible aspects of culture tend to treat it as a variable. In their perspective culture is something that an organization *has*. It is one of several organizational variables that can be controlled, managed, or changed once it is known. On the other hand authors who focus on the intangible aspects of culture tend to treat organizations as cultural settings. Organizations *are* cultures that need to be understood from a cultural perspective.

The Variable Perspective

In the managerial literature the *variable perspective* focuses on expressions of culture. These expressions may take the form of verbal and physical behaviors or practices, of artifacts, and of their underlying meanings. Advocates of this perspective draw selectively from Cultural Materialism, from Functionalism—

one area of symbolic anthropology—and from the behavioral sciences. They emphasize cultural manifestations that are tangible—whether behavioral, artifactual, or symbolic. It seems, however, that the focus on behavioral manifestations has its roots both in the training of managerial researchers as well as in a highly selective stream of anthropological literature. *Culture* is defined as "the way we do things here," or as manifestations of behavioral norms. The focus is placed on observable behavior. This behavior is predominantly inferred from data based on prestructured self-reports. Within this perspective culture is something that organizations have. Culture is treated as another organizational variable that may be controlled once it is known.

Anthropologists who promote a symbolic manifestation consider culture a system of shared symbols and meanings. By analogy some authors in the managerial literature refer to this perspective as "organizational symbolism."[20] Because managerial authors place the major focus of their research on the study of artifacts as expressions of culture, this stream of literature is subsumed under the manifestation-oriented perspective, even though the ultimate purpose for studying symbols or "symboling behavior" is close to the ideational perspective. Authors consider culture predominantly the product of symbolic operations—rather than social interactions—in which the manipulation of symbols and their attributed and shared meanings are prominent. They infer apparently shared meanings from the study of culturally expressive activities, behaviors, and material artifacts.

Of major interest are collective activities such as rites, rituals, and ceremonies as well as collective verbal behaviors such as language in general and, more specifically, speeches, jargon, stories, legends, myths, or humor. Material artifacts are taken as the tangible products or tools of culture. Examples are the thickness of a carpet, the treatment of physical space, or the available technology. These artifacts allow inferences about underlying meanings in their context when compared with meanings attributed to the same artifacts in other comparable settings.

The process of "deciphering" cultural manifestations is, however, difficult and involves some guesswork. Because researchers approach a study site with their own categories for perception, thought, and interpretation, errors and systematic biases are likely to occur.[21] To avoid these potential errors and to do justice to cultural aspects in a given context, the process of interpreting these context-specific meanings needs to be based on the insiders' logic, which they use to make sense out of their organizational reality including its manifestations. This implies unraveling a setting's own principles from an emic or insider view rather than from an etic or outsider perspective. Furthermore it implies a loop into the ideational or cognitive perspective.

The Cognitive Perspective

The *cognitive perspective* focuses on ideas, concepts, blueprints, beliefs, values, or norms that are seen as the core of the complex and multifaceted phenomenon called "culture." In anthropology and sociology these cognitive aspects of culture have also been described as "organized knowledge": the form of things that people have in their minds; their models for perceiving, integrating, and interpreting them; the ideas or theories that they use collectively to make sense of their social and physical reality. The anthropologist Keesing captures this perspective of culture well as the conceptual designs or the shared system of meaning that underlie the way people live. From this Cultural Idealism perspective, *culture* refers to what humans learn, what they have in their mind, and not what they do and make. This accumulated knowledge that is held collectively provides standards for deciding what is, for deciding what to do, and for deciding how to do things.[22]

In the managerial literature we can find this perspective of culture with various degrees of specificity and concreteness. Rather abstract versions are the collective programming of the human mind or the collective will of a corporate culture's members. Some authors refer to a set of shared understandings or meanings, to a system of publicly and collectively accepted meanings of a group, or a set of important understandings shared by a community. Others define *culture* as a set of shared values, as shared norms and expectations, as beliefs and expectations shared by most of the members of an organization's culture, or as assumptions commonly held by members of a group.[23]

Despite the wide range of concepts, there are some underlying commonalities within the ideational perspective. Culture in organizations is considered a social construction of rules that guide perceptions and thinking. It supplies the conceptual designs that provide standards for deciding what is, what to do about it, and how to go about it. These conceptual designs emerge in a process of social interaction that is primarily oriented toward problem solving. Over time a body of cultural knowledge is being created that is passed on to other generations. This view of culture applied to organizations is captured comprehensively in Schein's work. His perspective of culture reflects the influences of a social psychologist and of anthropologists who subscribe to a pattern as well as a utilitarian perspective of culture.

Schein (1984, p. 3) defines *organizational culture* as

the pattern of basic assumptions that a given group has invented, discovered, or developed in learning to cope with its problems of external adaptation and internal integration, and that have worked well enough to be considered valid, and, therefore, to be taught to new members as the correct way to perceive, think, and feel in relation to those problems.

Phillips[24] gives a similar, yet more concise, definition of *culture* in organizational settings, which does not draw as directly from the integration-oriented pattern view:

Culture is a set of assumptions commonly-held by a group of people. The set is distinctive to the group. The assumptions serve as guides to acceptable perceptions, thought, feeling, and behavior, are tacit among members, are learned and are passed on to each new member of the group.

Both the ideational and the manifestation-oriented perspective are responses to the problem of capturing the complex phenomenon called "culture." Similar to the field of anthropology, neither of them can, however, be considered the exclusive conception of culture in organizations. They focus on parts of culture from different angles. A combination of these two perspectives, such as the holistic view, may eventually render a comprehensive picture of culture in organizations. Unfortunately, little research has been conducted from this holistic perspective because it does not lend itself easily to research. Several authors have drawn attention to this problem. In their view such a holistic perspective lacks "analytical bite".[25] They suggest that culture should be considered a source of concepts such as images and ideas. These different concepts can then be studied in detail.

The fact that the ideational perspective has become the dominant view within the managerial literature does not mean that the concept of culture applied to organizations has become more clear or less ambiguous. Three major conceptual problems arise from an evaluation of the current literature.

PROBLEMS IN THE ORGANIZATIONAL LITERATURE

Current conceptions of culture in organizations have three major conceptual problems. One refers to the question about the components of culture that are only considered from a structural view. The second concerns the dimensions of culture in organizational settings. And the third relates to untested assumptions made about the concept of culture that may not be appropriate in its organizational setting.

What Are the Components of Culture?

Descriptions of culture focus variously on concepts such as ideologies, a coherent set of beliefs, the basic philosophy, basic assumptions, a set of core values, or a set of norms. The few studies that have been conducted do not help clarify this conceptual jungle; they only reflect the selective emphasis that is placed on any one of these concepts. Furthermore the use of these concepts seems, at times, arbitrary because some authors use, for example, *values* in the same way that others use *beliefs* or vice versa.

Can these concepts be substituted for one another given that researchers tend to focus on a single one when they talk about culture? Or do they stand for different ideational components? If so, which ones? It seems appropriate at this point to consider them all aspects of culture. However, this does not solve the problem of what they specifically mean. The meaning of *norms* as rules of behaviors is relatively clear but not the specific meanings of *values, beliefs,* and *assumptions.* Social psychologists have researched values more extensively than organizational scholars.[26] They define values in terms of enduring beliefs. Can beliefs then be substituted for values or do other beliefs exist in addition to enduring ones? And which values are most relevant in regard to culture in organizations? Brown[27] distinguishes, for example, between social values, managerial values, employee values, and business values.

Schein offers in his work a structural differentiation among the components of culture from a holistic perspective. He considers artifacts such as technology, art, and visible and audible behaviors located at the visible level of culture. They can be seen but are difficult to decipher. Values are located at a level that allows some awareness. He specifies them as espoused values that focus on what people say and think as reasons for their actions. Over time, as these values are reinforced through continued application, they turn into underlying assumptions. These assumptions are preconscious, invisible, and taken for granted. Schein considers them the actual reasons that underlie behavior, and his core definition of culture is only based on assumptions.

Differentiation into different levels clarifies the relation between the use of the terms *artifacts, values,* and *assumptions* by one author but not by others. Furthermore no guidelines exist for an unambiguous implementation of either values or basic assumptions. It seems reasonable at this stage of theory development to abandon these frequently used concepts that have been taken as substitutes for culture. It may be more fruitful to use generic constructs that directly reflect the underlying nature of the ideational components of culture.

The structural components of culture are interesting not only at one moment in time, they somehow emerge, develop, become institutionalized, and may change over time. While some authors recognize that the various components of culture are learned and passed on, only a few differentiate explicitly between a structural aspect and a developmental aspect including the respective interrelations. A comprehensive theory of culture in organizational settings should, however, include both structural aspects and their changing nature because, over time, organizations and their cultural realities go through various stages.[28] These arguments have led to the conceptualization that is presented in Chapter 3.

What Are the Dimensions of Culture?

In addition to the lack of clarity about the components of culture, confusion also exists about its dimensions. Different authors propound different dimensions as *the* dimensions or the most important dimensions of culture. Based on the work of Kluckhohn and Strodbeck, Schein[29] introduced five assumptions into the organizational literature as the basic assumptions of culture. They are the relation to the environment, the nature of reality, the nature of time and space, the nature of human nature, the nature of human activity, and the nature of human relationships.

Pümpin and Kobi and Wüthrich[30] consider seven orientations as relevant cultural dimensions: a firm's orientation to customers, employees, results, or achievements; to innovation; to productivity and costs; employees' orientation to the company; and the orientation to technology.

Deal and Kennedy[31] propose two independent dimensions that lead to four distinctly different corporate cultures: the degree of risk orientation and the speed of feedback on actions taken. Two independent dimensions are also assumed and used by Kilmann and Saxton,[32] whose work on culture focuses on an assessment of norms. One of their dimensions refers to a focus on people or technology ranging from technical to human, whereas the other one is a time dimension ranging from short term to long term.

The problem with these postulated dimensions is that they are set a priori. They make sense within their author's framework but then, again, several questions arise. Are two dimensions sufficient to characterize culture? Are five or seven more appropriate? And if so, which ones? The only suggestion that seems to be appropriate on the basis of the existing literature is a contingent one: Different dimensions may be more relevant for different purposes. Which dimensions of culture are, however, more relevant under what kind of conditions cannot be decided merely on theoretical grounds. Basic research needs to address this issue.

What Are Appropriate Assumptions About Culture in Organizational Settings?

In addition to the conceptual confusion about the components and dimensions of culture, untested assumptions exist about certain characteristics of culture. These assumptions may, however, not be appropriate. They are either adopted from anthropology without attention to the differences in context, or they are based on managerial preconceptions and research practices. Two of the most widely shared assumptions in the managerial literature are that culture in organizations is (a) homogeneous and shared among organizational members and (b) leader generated and leader centered. These two points will be examined more closely.

Is culture homogeneous? The assumption about a *homogeneous culture* is directly reflected in the two terms *organizational culture* and *corporate culture*. The assumption has been imported selectively, and without reflection, from anthropology. Anthropologists' focal point of research has predominantly been small-scale societies. They have mostly studied isolated, small, and homogeneous tribes that have relatively simple forms of organizational arrangements to regulate their community life as compared with today's organizations.

Most of today's organizations and their relevant environments are more complex, more dynamic, and less isolated. The multiple interdependencies that exist between an organization and its relevant environment increase the level of complexity further. Being open, adaptive, or even proactive to change is today a capacity vital to an organization's survival. Firms need to be aware of the actions of their competitors. They need to anticipate and respond to changing customer needs. They need to accommodate the changing values and needs of their work forces. They need to be sensitive to changing societal values such as increased awareness of environmental pollution. They need to be responsive to political, economic, and legal changes. And they need to stay in touch with technological developments that may affect their operations or their customers' requests. In addition the situation is further complicated for firms operating internationally, multinationally, or globally. And larger-scale organizations consist of multiple subsystems and work groups to deal with various requirements imposed by their external business environments. These consist of people who are potential carriers of multiple types of cultural knowledge and who most likely belong to several cultural groups.

Organizational members are usually members of different task, work, or problem-solving groups inside and outside their work organizations. They have been raised and socialized within a particular society, which may not have been the same nation, or the same social stratum within one nation, for all of them. Each organizational member is simultaneously a member of a societal subculture, a specific geographical region, an ethnic group, a religious group, a professional group, an age group, and a gender group, among others. It is quite unlikely that all members of an organization hold congruent memberships across these and other groupings.

Simultaneous membership in different groups does not necessarily mean that the associated roles all have the same level of importance to a person at a given point in time. Depending on the tasks, issues, and work-related or personal problems at hand, a different role, different involvements and different concerns, will be more salient, including a set of knowledge and expectations that come with it. They may differ for people who work in the same organization and may be reflected in heterogeneous cultural knowledge.

The results of two studies support the notion that organizational or corporate culture is less monolithic than assumed. In an ethnoscientific study of professionals in the Silicon Valley, Gregory[33] identified distinct cultures of professionals that are not simply subcultures, dominated by an organization's culture, but that cut across several organizations. Individuals identified more strongly with their particular profession than with the company for which they were working.

The results of another study suggest the existence of subcultures within an organization in terms of hierarchy and function. The researchers interviewed a random sample of 64 employees stratified according to tenure, hierarchy, and function. In a structured, open-ended interview format, events were explored that were considered important for the company's future. While tenure did not make a difference in the recollections and interpretations of events, a detailed analysis of the findings indicated that organizational members tend to focus on their own hierarchic level as well as on the functions they perform.[34]

The results of the two studies do, unfortunately, not conclusively answer questions about the kinds of subcultures that may exist in an organization. They challenge, however, the assumptions about organizational or corporate culture as a monolithic entity that are supported by the sociological literature. This leads to the question about what kind of subcultures may emerge and exist in an organization.

Is culture leader generated and leader centered? The presumption of a monolithic culture is due, in part, to a second assumption frequently held about culture in organizations: the assumption that culture is leader generated and leader centered, which originated in some early managerial literature that is often cited by authors writing about organizational culture. But this bias also results from researchers' predominant focus on top management.

One of the most frequently cited books in the early literature on organizational culture is Philip Selznick's *Leadership in Administration*. Selznick[35] attributes the maintenance of an organization, its institutionalization, to the leader as he or she infuses the organization with values. This process of infusing values into an organization is considered crucial for its formation of a distinct character. This process is the parallel of a person's character formation. While authors argue in the more recent literature that culture comes into existence at the birth of an organization, most of them seem to agree with Selznick that the founder and leader is the major force in shaping, maintaining, and perpetuating culture in an organization.

In addition authors in the managerial literature have a bias toward top management, often for practical reasons. Top management is most likely to give successful access and entry to a company, and its members constitute the desired audience of popular management books. Furthermore many researchers and practitioners believe that interventions and changes have to originate and be driven by the top. A focus on top management is, therefore, desirable because it is practical: Access and remaining in a company for research purposes is made easier and the level and focus of analysis are well defined. Hence the resulting research efforts are less messy and complex. In addition, it is management's desire to control the company, including employees' behaviors.

These reasons help us understand why there is a prominent focus on the founder, leader, and top management. The question arises, however, on whether the top management's perspective cascades through an entire organization. If not, the results obtained from a study with a top management focus cannot be generalized to an entire organization. Rather than reflecting the culture of an organization, they may solely reflect the subculture of the top management. Top management may be dissociated from the organization's operational base. They may think that their views are widely held throughout the company when, in reality, they are not. The limited focus on top management is, therefore, considered premature at this point because too little empirical knowledge is available. Future research needs to include all levels of an organization to determine the degree of influence that a founder, leader(s), or top management have on the various aspects of culture in their processes of formation, maintenance, perpetuation, and change. This was one of the issues addressed in this study.

SUMMARY

We can summarize the above criticism in three arguments:

(1) There is no consensus in the literature about what the components of culture are from an ideational perspective. Several concepts have been used to refer to culture such as philosophies, ideas, values, beliefs, or norms. These concepts have, however, been used imprecisely with little or no indication of how they can be studied. In a study of culture within organizational contexts, it seems, therefore, more fruitful to set these concepts aside and use instead more generic constructs that capture the structural and dynamic characteristics of culture in organizations.

(2) Several dimensions of culture have been postulated a priori by different authors without questioning whether these dimensions are either appropriate or comprehensive within

organizational settings. I have argued that relevant dimensions of culture should emerge empirically rather than being pre-imposed.

(3) Culture in organizations has been widely assumed to be a homogeneous entity and leader centered. The first assumption may not hold in complex organizations. And the second one most likely reflects a bias of managerial researchers. It is also necessary to generate more empirically based knowledge in this regard, and I suggest examination of the cultural dynamics and the potential existence of cultural groupings. This implies, however, that top management is not the sole focus for data collection.

To overcome the shortcomings of current conceptualizations of culture in organizational settings and to tackle the problems discussed above, I have developed a conception of culture in terms of cultural knowledge. This conception is based on the cognitive perspective of culture in organizational settings.

NOTES

1. Malinowski (1939) and Chase (1948).
2. Peters (1984).
3. Langness (1979).
4. The interested reader is referred to Adelung (1773), Herder (1784), or Knigge (1788/1977).
5. Tylor (1871/1958, Vol. 1).
6. Kroeber and Kluckhohn (1952).
7. Hatch (1973) shows, for example, how the different interests of anthropologists have guided their research and led to different foci in research and theory.
8. For a more detailed discussion, see, for example, Hatch (1973) and Langness (1979).
9. See, for example, Tylor (1871/1958); other representatives of cultural evolution are Adelung (1773) or Lubbock (1879/1912).
10. See, for example, Campbell (1966) or Freeman (1970).
11. Boas (1896).
12. Kroeber (1917) and Benedict (1934).
13. Sapir (1917).
14. Lévi-Strauss (1949).
15. Herskovits (1924), LeVine (1954), and Mair (1934) studied, for example, tribes in Africa. Meggit (1965) studied tribes in New Guinea and Mead (1939), and Radcliffe-Brown (1922) investigated peoples living on isolated islands.

16. Teenagers were studied by Kruse (1975), cocktail waitresses by Spradley and Mann (1975), groups in the urban community by Gans (1967) and White (1943), and the sense-making processes of judges by Garfinkel (1967).

17. Lipp (1979).

18. Goodenough, W. H. (1957): Cultural anthropology and linguistics. In: P. Carving (Ed.), *Report of the Seventh Annual Round Table on Linguistics and Language Study*. Washington, D.C., Georgetown University.

19. This perspective is described in more detail in Kluckhohn (1951) and Kroeber and Kluckhohn (1952).

20. See, for example, Berg (1983).

21. Kaplan (1964) discusses these issues further.

22. See, for example, Keesing (1974); Keesing & Keesing, (1971).

23. Peters and Waterman (1982) focus, for example, on values; Allen (1984), Kilmann and Saxton (1983), and Silverzweig and Allen (1976) focus on norms; while Sapienza (1985) emphasizes beliefs and Schein (1983) assumptions.

24. Phillips (1984).

25. See, for example, Pettigrew (1979) and Preszeworski and Teune (1970).

26. See, for example, Rokeach (1975).

27. Brown (1976).

28. Kimberly and Miles (1980) discuss the changing nature of organizations as they move through different life cycles. These life cycles are most likely accompanied by different cultural realities as discussed in Sackmann (1983).

29. Kluckhohn and Strodbeck (1961) and Schein (1984).

30. Pümpin (1984) and Kobi and Wüthrich (1986).

31. Deal and Kennedy (1982).

32. Kilmann and Saxton (1983).

33. Gregory (1983).

34. Martin, Sitkin, and Boehm (1983).

35. Selznick (1957).

THREE

An Alternative Conception of Culture in Organizations

Instead of selecting one or several of the concepts that have been used to refer to culture in the organizational and managerial literature, I decided to choose "generic" constructs that reflect the underlying nature of culture. In the tradition of the cognitive perspective,[1] the *sense-making mechanisms* are of particular interest, and they are those mechanisms that organizational members use to attribute meanings to events. These mechanisms include the standards and rules for perceiving, interpreting, believing, and acting that are typically used in a given cultural setting. Within this perspective artifacts and behavioral manifestations are considered expressions of culture. These expressions are located at the visible surface level while their attached meanings are below the visible level. Their understanding requires an inquiry into the underlying processes of sense-making.[2]

Based on the underlying commonalities of these sense-making mechanisms, the essence of culture can be conceptualized as the collective construction of social reality. Sense making is a complicated, holistic process in which perception, existing knowledge, and judgments interact with each other. These, in turn, influence actions, perceptions, judgments, and thinking.

People use cognitive structuring devices, or *cognitions*, to attribute meaning to events. Thus the *structural* side of culture can be defined as

> sets of commonly held cognitions that are *held with some emotional investment* and integrated into a logical system or cognitive map that contains cognitions about *descriptions, operations, prescriptions,* and *causes.* They are *habitually used* and influence perception, thinking, feeling, and acting.

The structural components of culture are present at any point in time. The cultural *content* may vary, however, depending on its development. Hence this structural perspective needs to be complemented by a developmental perspective. This *developmental* perspective addresses the formation, change, and perpetuation of cultural cognitions over time in the form of cultural knowledge:

> Cognitions become commonly held in processes of social interaction. They can be introduced into the organization based on outside experiences, they can emerge from growing experiences, they can be invented and/or negotiated. In repeated applications they *become attached with emotions and assigned with degrees of importance*—also commonly held. They are *relatively stable over time* and accumulated in the form of different kinds of cultural knowledge that are labeled dictionary, directory, recipe, and axiomatic knowledge. This cultural knowledge is *passed on* to new members.

I now explain the various components of this definition in more detail. It draws upon cognitive and social psychology. Furthermore it integrates those aspects of the culture concept's sociological and anthropological roots that apply under conditions of complex organizational settings.

Cognitions are sets of categories that guide perception and thinking. Individuals use them to perceive, classify, and interpret perceived phenomena according to the meanings assigned to them. Cognitions hence help people to construct and understand reality. They are interrelated and integrated into a logical system or cognitive map.[3] Four structural aspects of a cognitive map are relevant to culture in organizations. These are descriptive categories ("what is"), their interrelations and integrations in the form of causal-analytical attributions ("how"), and causal-normative attributions ("should") as well as ultimate explanations about "why" certain things happen.

Descriptive components contain *definitions* and *descriptions* of phenomena. The potential meanings that may be attributed to a specific setting or event are reduced to the one that collectively makes most sense to the people of a particular cultural setting. These definitions and descriptions describe "what is." To give an example, if the term *innovation* is used in a manufacturing company such as 3M, it is most likely interpreted as *product innovation.* And if asked for one of the firm's most important innovations, organizational members will probably name one of the product innovations such as "Post-It." If the same term *innovation* is used in a service-based industry, it is much more likely to be interpreted in terms of a process innovation. In a consulting firm the most important innovation may be seen in the firm's specific way of interacting with clients rather than in its specific service products.

These descriptive components represent lexical knowledge. I have labeled its accumulation *dictionary knowledge.* This kind of cultural knowledge describes the slice of organizational reality that is considered relevant in a given cultural setting by its members. In the firm in which I did research, several people considered as one of its major innovations, for example, a particular strategy. Their specific strategy was interpreted as "controlled profitable growth" with the following characteristics: selling unprofitable divisions, making profitable sales, expanding existing markets, providing additional customer services, identifying additional niches, giving employees autonomy in their actions, improving quality controls, or improving the existing telephone system. In another firm organizational members may not consider its strategy to be a major innovation. And, if probed about what their strategy is, they may give a different characterization even if the same term *strategy* is used.

Causal-analytical attributions are *expectations about cause-and-effect relationships* in actual occurrences. These causal attributions refer to the operational aspects of events, practices, and processes. They describe perceived causal relations among events, their chain of actions. Taken together they reflect a logic of perceived actions and the respective outcomes. To give an example, if a situation is interpreted as "we need to produce a new part," a series of action steps follow. These have usually proven successful in similar situations. This knowledge and past experience guide specific actions such as sequencing of production, materials used for production, the time and care taken in producing that part, and so on.

Causal-analytical attributions represent commonly held theories of actions labeled *directory knowledge*, which contains information on "how to" do something. It has a descriptive rather than evaluative quality. In the researched firm the existing directory knowledge described, for example, how people interact with each other "properly" as defined within their cultural setting or how a problem is usually solved. In the latter case all those who are concerned with the problem get together and discuss the situation. Each individual is expected to contribute with his or her special skills, to initiate, and to take responsibility for actions that are within his or her domain of work. Whenever necessary these individual activities culminate in team efforts.

Causal-normative attributions are cause-and-effect relationships of hypothetical events. They reflect recommendations for improvements and repairs. They constitute prescriptive theories of action. They refer to what should or should not be done when one is faced with a specific issue—how one should improve things or what one should do differently to improve. They represent an evaluation and judgment of actions and their outcomes. The following is an example of a typical statement: "We should do XYZ to improve the quality of this product." I have labeled the accumulation of causal-normative attributions *recipe knowledge.*

Recipe knowledge comes close to "wisdom": It represents prescriptive recommendations based on collective experiences and judgments. It contains recipes for survival and success. With this prescriptive quality, recipe knowledge is closely related to norms. Typical recipes are "to survive in this firm, one has to duck at the right moment," "never challenge your boss," "a good leader yells," or "a product with poor quality should never leave the plant." In the firm under investigation little recipe knowledge could be found. Further probing revealed that the lack of recipe knowledge was typical for the cultural environment of the firm. Thus the amount of cultural knowledge that exists in a particular setting reveals additional aspects about its cultural qualities.

Different cognitions are initially of equal importance. Depending on personal or collective preferences, past experiences, and/or the number of successful applications, different *emphases* or *priorities* emerge among the cognitions. People assign different degrees of importance to them. The aspect of emphasis cuts across all three kinds of cultural knowledge and highlights their most prominent aspects. While the different kinds of knowledge may be quite elaborate in a given organization, the strongly emphasized ones—those of the highest priority—are considered the best indicators for understanding an organization's specific cultural context. Little or no emphasis give additional contrasting insights.

Degrees of importance may also change over time. To give an example from the study, the firm under investigation had just completed a major restructuring process. Before, during, and after the restructuring process, its organizational structure was a major issue for management. Before the restructuring they emphasized centralization with all its consequences. During and after the reorganization they attempted to achieve and keep the highest possible level of decentralization throughout the firm. This example shows how priorities and emphasis may change radically over time within the same setting.

In each cultural setting, ultimate explanations exist referring to "why" certain events happen. These basic reasons cannot be further reduced. They represent the final causes just like axioms in mathematics. They are set a priori and can be compared with religion. Their ultimate existence is based on fundamental beliefs, or "philosophical discussions" as the president of the researched firm characterized it. I have labeled the accumulation of these final causes *axiomatic knowledge*. Examples of axiomatic knowledge are explanations about why a certain strategy is chosen, why a certain organizational structure is preferred over another, why it is important to hire and promote certain people, why a specific way of interacting and dealing with each other is considered important, or what kind of people are preferred as employees.

A cognitive map—the integration of the four kinds of cultural knowledge and the respective priorities—represents an experientially developed theory for understanding, explanation, and prediction. It is an everyday or layman's theory that people in a particular cultural setting use as a reference for their orientation and guidance. Hence this knowledge structure influences their way of thinking, feeling, and acting. Over time this—structural—cognitive map is filled with context-specific experiences that transform it into a *cultural knowledge map*. Table 3.1 provides the reader with an overview of the different kinds of knowledge, their definition, and their integration into a cultural knowledge map.

In general cognitions are neutral sense-making, planning, and acting devices that are individually held. What makes them cultural is the aspect of *collectivity* and the kind of emotional attachment that goes with it. Individuals draw on those frames of reference that they have learned and acquired over the years. These may have emerged in different socialization processes: within the family, growing up in a specific region and country, belonging to a certain ethnic group, having experienced a certain kind of education and professional training, and working in a specific firm. The firm's socialization is only one of several cultural reference groups. How can one then distinguish whether a person draws on his or her individual socialization processes or on the firm's cultural knowledge base?

Table 3.1 The Cultural Knowledge Map: Definitions and Characteristics of the Different Kinds of Cultural Knowledge

CENTRALISM/IMPORTANCE (high → low)

ACCUMULATION of Cultural Knowledge (time)

KINDS of Cultural Knowledge	COGNITIVE COMPONENTS	CHARACTERISTIC QUESTION	MANIFESTATIONS
DICTIONARY KNOWLEDGE	descriptive categories	"what is" "that exists"	difinitions and labels of things and events
DIRECTORY KNOWLEDGE	causal-analytical attributions	"how are things done"	expectations about cause & effect relationships, descriptive theory of action
RECIPE KNOWLEDGE	causal-normative attribution	"should" "ought to"	cause & effect relationships of hypothetical events prescriptive theory of action
AXIOMATIC KNOWLEDGE	causes, assumptions/axioms	"why things are done the way they are"	fundamental beliefs

39

Cultural cognitions are *simultaneously* held by several individuals. They are no longer property or characteristics of one single person. Instead they are part of the collectivity—even if they are held individually. Cultural cognitions go beyond the individual, they can outlive individuals, or, as White[4] expresses it, they are located in an "extrasomatic" rather than an "intrasomatic" context. People who carry these cultural cognitions do not have to be aware of the fact that others hold the same cognitions. Thus, for an outsider, cultural cognitions are apparently shared. We refer to those who hold the same or similar cognitions about a specific issue as a *cultural grouping* in terms of this issue.

The plural form in "sets of commonly held cognitions" implies the possible existence of several cultural groupings. A cultural grouping is not restricted to formal membership or physical presence in a group. Instead it may consist of individuals located in different places within and across the physical boundaries of an organization. What makes a collection of people a cultural grouping is the fact that the people hold the same cognitions in common. The boundaries of cultural groupings are, therefore, flexible; they may shift. And the membership in one cultural grouping may just be one of several for a person. Because individuals have several frames of reference at their disposal, the salience of these frames may change depending on the issue at hand. If I am a highly committed member of my profession, my work group, and the firm, I may nevertheless decide to stay at home if my child is sick. In this instance the reference group "family" is suddenly more important than the reference group "firm" or "work group." Or I may decide to skip an important work group meeting in favor of a professional conference. In this decision my professional identity is more salient than my work group identity.

This last notion differentiates cultural groupings from the existing concept of subcultures as found in the traditional literature. Subcultures are usually associated with clear-cut boundaries. These are set a priori in regard to a specific variable such as department, function, profession, hierarchy, or ethnicity. As such subcultures are treated as homogeneous and rather closed entities. The more traditional conceptions of sub-culture do not acknowledge the idea that several overlapping subcultures may exist. Such a view seems, however, more appropriate for complex organizational systems. In addition the findings of two studies support such multiple, overlapping membership.[5]

Commonly held cognitions are *socially created*, maintained, changed, and perpetuated. They emerge in the process of joint problem solving in which meanings are negotiated. Cultural cognitions represent recognized solutions or impasses to the resolution of perceived tasks or problems. Solutions that are developed by one individual can become cultural when others adopt them. A growing number of people start using them as descriptions, operations, prescriptions, or causes for successful or unsuccessful activities. Current members pass them on to new members through their verbal and nonverbal behavior. As such these cognitions are likely to outlive their creators.

In the process of repeated applications, these cognitions become *imbued with emotions*, and *degrees of importance* are assigned to them. Their users like them if they lead to successful results and dislike them if they lead to negative results. Members of a group begin to associate them with specific sanctioning behavior, feelings of belonging, or psychological security. In their repeated use certain kinds of cultural cognitions—by then part of the cultural knowledge—will be perceived as having more importance than others. They are more emphasized. Their use varies with the frequency of recurring tasks, issues, and problems and their perceived importance. The magnitude and range of implications for the company influences perceived importance. In this process cultural cognitions and knowledge also become *habits*—habits of thought that translate into habitual actions. Once they exist the carriers of cultural knowledge apply them without prior reflection when faced with a specific situation.

The various aspects of cultural knowledge about past successes and failures are communicated to and *learned* by new members, who may also import cultural variety into the organization. This acquired knowledge becomes generalized in successive communication and reinforcement processes. Eventually its carriers perceive the knowledge as having a higher degree of factuality than originally existed. The process of passing on has, to some extent, inertia and time lag built in because the knowledge is based in the past. The resulting body of cultural knowledge may, therefore, become dissociated from its original meanings over time. This process is comparable to the development of rumors.[6] In successive communication a piece of information becomes embellished and changed because every person attributes something to it from his or her own frames of reference.

The cultural cognitions and their respective maps are relatively *stable over time*. They constitute a commonly held logic or everyday theory that is constantly reinforced by its carriers' successful applications. Once such a cultural knowledge structure exists, it is more likely to become further differentiated rather than being replaced or exchanged. Research has shown, for example, that we tend to reject or negate single invalidating experiences. We refute them as exceptions to the rule or attribute their existence to other causes.[7]

Cultural cognitions—and eventually a cultural knowledge map—have functional attributes. They create a common basis for perception, thinking, feeling, and acting among their carriers. This basis helps individuals to recognize, frame, and integrate meaningful alternatives from an essentially infinite number of possibilities in similar ways. This capacity is a prerequisite for mutual understanding, for communication, and for effective coordination in social systems. Cultural cognitions may serve as integrators within and across structural divisions. In doing so they complement the shortcomings and gray areas of an organization's formal structure. In this respect cultural cognitions and cultural knowledge provide an invisible bond among their possessors. This functional aspect does not reveal, however, to what extent they are appropriate for a specific organization to conduct its business most effectively. Only a comparison with the demands and requirements placed upon the organization can reveal their appropriateness.

Another aspect of this basis for mutual understanding and bond among its members is its complexity reduction. When faced with a complex situation, the available cultural knowledge structure guides individuals in their unreflected decisions about what is important and what is not, what is considered a problem and what is not, what is appropriate behavior and what is inappropriate in a specific cultural setting, or what is acceptable and what is unacceptable. In one cultural setting it may be acceptable and expected of an employee to run into the boss's office if he or she has a problem. In another cultural setting the same behavior may be considered unacceptable because problems should be solved where they occur. And only if the employee does not find a solution is he or she allowed to bring it to his or her boss. Or, when faced with the same problems, people in different cultural settings may respond completely differently. Sapienza[8] found, for example, in her research that the top management of two different hospitals interpreted the same legal change quite differently. One group saw new opportunities while the other felt boxed in when faced with the same environmental change. The subsequent actions of the two groups differed respectively.

This conception of the essence of culture as sets of commonly held cognitions (structural) and cultural knowledge (developmental) was applied in the study that I designed to examine the comprehensiveness and usefulness of this conceptualization. In addition, I wanted to gain a better understanding of the nature of culture in organizational settings. More specifically the research project addressed the following questions:

- To what extent is the proposed conceptualization of cultural knowledge appropriate for understanding the cultural context of an organization?
- Which are the relevant structural components of cultural knowledge in organizational settings?
- What are the dynamic characteristics of cultural knowledge, that is, the processes of creating and maintaining it?
- What kind of cultural groupings may emerge in an organization and where are they located?

To address these questions I first had to develop an appropriate methodology. On the one hand I wanted to understand the cultural setting from an insider's perspective without spending the next five years in the research setting. On the other hand I wanted to obtain information that was also relevant beyond the immediate context of the firm. This dilemma implied that I needed a methodology which could strike a balance between an in-depth ethnography and a "quick and dirty" questionnaire study.

The "midrange" methodology that I finally used could strike such a balance. Its major components are a design of successive comparisons that allowed a step-wise progression from an initial exploratory stage to final testing of a hypothesis that emerged in regard to the formation of cultural groupings; an unstructured interviewing procedure that combined a phenomenological orientation with an issue focus, with "innovation" as the chosen issue; theoretical content analysis of the obtained interview data; observations during the interviews and in the research sites as well as documentary analysis—both were used to validate or discard the information obtained in the interviews—and critical discussions with two informed colleagues during the entire research process and a feedback session with top management which served as a reality test.

As research sites I selected a U.S. firm with headquarters and several divisions in the Los Angeles area. I collected data from three different sites of the firm: from the headquarters—including top management—and from people across all hierarchic levels and functional areas of two of the firm's divisions. Both divisions had belonged to the firm for approximately the same number of years. The reader who is interested in the details of the developed methodology, research sites, research process, and data analyses will find them described in Appendix A: Methodology.

The following chapter gives a synopsis of the major findings of the study before I discuss them in detail in Chapters 5 to 8.

NOTES

1. Some authors refer to this as the "interpretative perspective."

2. This perspective has roots in cognitive anthropology (i.e., Goodenough, 1971), in semiotics (i.e., Geertz, 1973), in ethnography (i.e., Garfinkel, 1967), in phenomenology (Husserl, 1948/1928, 1975; Schütz, 1945, 1962), in the social constructionist view of organizational life (i.e., Berger & Luckmann, 1966; Parsons & Shils, 1951; Silverman, 1971: Weick, 1979), and in cognitive psychology (i.e., Foa & Foa, 1974; Kelly, 1979; Schank & Abelson, 1977; Taylor & Fiske, 1981).

3. The concept "cognitive map" is taken from cognitive psychology. It was first used by Tolman (1948) in his study of rats' behavior in mazes and has since been applied to the human mind. It refers to the cognitive structure that is compared in its totality with the structure and content of a geographic map.

4. White (1959).

5. These two studies were conducted by Gregory (1983) and Martin, Sitkin, and Boehm (1983).

6. Rosnow and Fine (1976) discuss, for example, the development of rumors.

7. The interested reader is referred to Sherif, Sherif, and Nebergall (1965) or Weiner (1980).

8. Sapienza (1985).

FOUR

A Preview: Insights Into the Nature of Cultural Knowledge

This chapter provides an overview of the major insights that were gained from the study, both in regard to theory and methodology. The respective results are then described and discussed in detail in the regular chapters. In general the results of the study provide answers to the questions presented previously and give further insights into the nature of culture in organizational settings. The developed conception of the essence of culture in terms of different kinds of cultural knowledge and different types of cognitions proved to be comprehensive and useful. I was able to capture the essence of the cultural context of the investigated company. Furthermore the study gives detailed information about axiomatic knowledge, which I had originally not included in the conception. This axiomatic knowledge reveals basic guidelines that were deliberately put in place during a major restructuring phase of the company.

The midrange methodology that I developed was useful in various ways. Its focal method for data collection—the issue-focused interviewing technique with the phenomenological orientation—was sensitive to cultural knowledge. It prompted respondents to think and reflect about what they considered important company innovations, why they consider them to be important, and how they had came about. The term *innovation* was, however, too abstract for people at lower levels. *Innovation* was, therefore, rephrased in terms of important changes that had occurred in the company.

I argued above that corporate or organizational culture may not be as homogeneous and monolithic as some authors assume. Overall the findings of this research both support and contradict the existence of a homogeneous or single culture within an organizational setting. The results indicate that culture in organizational settings needs to be viewed and treated in a more complex way than it has been up to now. The findings also suggest that a mere qualitative distinction between the four different kinds of cultural knowledge does not suffice. The qualitative distinction needs to be complemented with information about the specific structure of the different kinds of knowledge. In addition I received information about the factors that influence specific interpretations of cultural knowledge.

Analysis of the data revealed that the structure of cultural knowledge differs across the different kinds of knowledge. On the one hand a monolithic type of culture—a sort of cultural synergism—emerged across organizational members and divisions. But, at the same time, cultural groupings existed. Both of them—cultural synergism and cultural groupings—were found to exist simultaneously in regard to different kinds of cultural knowledge.

Table 4.1 summarizes findings on the various aspects of cultural knowledge. The table includes the different kinds of cultural knowledge and the boundaries that I identified in the study for cultural groupings. It also lists some crucial variables that tend to influence the content aspect of cultural groupings and their knowledge as well as some factors that I found maintain cultural groupings and their knowledge.

The various analyses of the data suggest that, in regard to *dictionary knowledge*—the descriptive aspect of cultural knowledge—cultural groupings exist according to functional domains. *Functional domain* is defined as the totality of intended and perceived functions that an organizational member

Table 4.1 A Summary of the Major Findings: The Kinds of Cultural Knowledge, Boundaries for Cultural Groupings, Variables Influencing the Content of Cultural Knowledge, and Factors Maintaining Cultural Groupings and Their Knowledge

Kinds of Cultural Knowledge	Boundaries for Cultural Groupings	Variables Influencing the Content of Cultural Groupings and Their Knowledge	Factors Maintaining Cultural Groupings and Their Knowledge
Recipe knowledge (do, don't, should)	Personal concerns Functional domains Division/Organization	Hierarchic levels Nature of employees Nature of work	Degree of autonomy Selection procedure Organization design
Dictionary knowledge (what)	Functional domains	Hierarchic levels Divisional boundaries Nature of work	Incentive and reward systems Organizational design Control systems
Directory knowledge (how)	Organizationwide	Nature of employees' beliefs and experience of the new president and corporate officers	Organizational design Organizational control mechanism Selection procedure
Axiomatic knowledge (why)	Top management	Personal beliefs of the new president negotiated with other corporate officers	Role modeling/mentorship Control through selection Symbolic rewards

performs and refers to a person's perceived responsibilities. Specific interpretation of a person's functional domain is influenced by hierarchy, by divisional identity, and—especially at lower levels—by the nature of the work.

Functional domains that are located at a higher level of the company's hierarchy are more "design" oriented whereas functional domains located at a lower level in the company's hierarchy are more "execution" oriented. *Design orientation* refers to the notion of creating intentions or plans. Organizational members create and develop general ideas about certain things such as specific policies and strategies that should be observed by all company members. *Execution orientation* refers to the realization of those intentions. In this process intentions are materialized and rendered real. Execution reveals the various impacts, consequences, and implications of a specific intention. The lower a functional domain grouping is located within the company's hierarchic structure, the more specific are these realizations of the respective intentions. Realizations are tied to the grouping's local, immediate concerns without necessarily revealing the general ideas or intentions that underlie specific realizations.

Seven groupings emerged within the three divisions of the company that I investigated: a design and control grouping at the top management level; two managerial marketing groupings, one in the PC and one in the GA division; a coordination grouping and three different production groupings in the PC division. Organizational design, incentive, and reward systems as well as other organizational control mechanisms were found to be the prominent factors in maintaining the different cultural groupings.

Regarding the *content* of dictionary knowledge, four major themes and one rudimentary one emerged from the data. Organizational members emphasized these themes across cultural groupings to different extents. Based on their predominant content, I labeled the themes *goal and accomplishments, strategy, structure, orientation toward organizational members,* and *physical work environment.*

The findings on different cultural groupings according to functional domains are not surprising. Neither is the influence of hierarchy in their interpretations. Even though no empirical support exists in the managerial literature for this manner of grouping, the cultural grouping mechanism reflects common-sense knowledge. The resulting groupings mirror the underlying rationale of organizational design by which companies are organized into departments according to different functions. Several authors suggest that employees who perform different functions and belong to different departments hold different views and distinct perspectives on certain issues. Burns[1] differentiates, for example, between a scientific and a managerial culture. And Handy[2] suggests that cultures of power, role, task, and person should be expected both at an organizational and at a departmental level.[3] In addition, personal experiences in organizations tend to support this finding. The major difference between these theoretical prescriptions and my findings is, however, that "functional domain" reflects an individual's active seizing of responsibilities, whereas "function," as treated in the literature, refers to a firm's prescribed roles for individuals.

An impact of hierarchy on cultural knowledge is suggested in the research of Martin, Sitkim, and Boehm.[4] Their data indicate that hierarchic position may have an effect on employees' knowledge of their company's history, even though the researchers expected tenure to show a significant difference. The authors' sample size was, however, too small to further examine their findings by conducting post hoc comparisons. Furthermore they investigated only the dictionary aspect of cultural knowledge. Thus the potential existence of other kinds of cultural knowledge such as operational or normative knowledge was neglected.

A comparison of the findings in regard to dictionary knowledge with the findings about *directory knowledge* is, however, surprising. Based on the cultural groupings that exist in regard to dictionary knowledge, one may expect to find the same cultural groupings. However, at the directory level of knowledge—which is cultural knowledge about processes, about how things get done—subcultures do not form according to functional domain. Analysis of directory information reveals "cultural synergism" instead of cultural groupings.

Cultural synergism is a term used to capture similarity in the structural processes that underlie the various actions of organizational members. These similarities exist even though the respective individuals may act independently of each other within the same or different locations of the company. That is, cultural groupings that exist according to functional domains in regard to dictionary knowledge could not be found in regard to directory knowledge. No matter what was named as major innovations, some of the underlying structural processes by which these different innovations were achieved were basically the same. This similarity runs across organizational members and across different cultural groupings. The boundaries for cultural groupings at this level enclosed all three research sites and can be hypothesized to be company wide.

I identified four common structural processes in regard to directory knowledge. Organizational members consider these four processes to be important. Given their nature I labeled them *task accomplishment, relationships among people, adaptation and change,* and *acquisition and perpetuation of knowledge.* Tasks are accomplished through a combination of individual and team efforts. People relate in very informal, direct, and open ways with each other. Within the firm special processes are in place for adaptation and change and for acquiring and perpetuating knowledge. Furthermore the data suggest that these four processes exist because of two conditions, which are the *specific nature of organizational members* and the *company's design.* Both conditions are, in fact, *pre*conditions for the structural processes in regard to directory knowledge. They represent deliberate choices by the top management of the company. They emerged from assumptions that the members of the top management group had negotiated. Top management used them as an a priori basis to guide a fundamental restructuring process of their company.

The analysis of *recipe information* which was defined as knowledge about what should be or should have been done to make things better indicate that this definition needs to be further differentiated. This kind of knowledge seems to consist of two aspects: recipes of success or failure which have a "continue to do" or "avoid to do" nature and recipes *for* success which show the originally expected and defined "should" nature. One recipe of success emerged across functional domains, hierarchical and divisional boundaries. I labeled it *action vs. talking about action*. It represents a strong recommendation to improve rather than suggest improvements. Three recipes for success surfaced which I labeled *time frame, approach to change*, and *problem areas*. The first one implies that decisions and their implementation should happen faster in BIND. The second one recommends a less cautious behavior toward change, and the third one delineates specific areas of concern which should change.

These recipes for success tended to be held in functional domain groupings and/or within divisional boundaries. Hierarchy, the nature of employees, and the nature of work seem to influence the content of cultural groupings and their knowledge. While the degree of autonomy varies among organizational members, BIND's careful selection of people and its organizational design tend to maintain the groupings and their knowledge. Thus the findings in regard to recipes of success and failure are closer to the ones in regard to directory knowledge whereas the findings about recipes for success are closer to the ones about dictionary knowledge.

In general, only few information surfaced in regard to recipe knowledge when compared to the other kinds of cultural knowledge because of the specific nature of BIND and its employees. These results are therefore the most tentative ones.

A historical and evolutionary—rather than structural—perspective revealed *axiomatic knowledge*. This information gives insights into the some of the basic reasons *why* certain things are the way they are in the company. Axiomatic knowledge was originally not included in the proposed conceptualization of cultural knowledge. Analysis of the interview data indicates, however, that it is an important part of the cultural knowledge base. Axiomatic knowledge becomes relevant if one is interested in the origins of cultural knowledge. More specifically it became clear from this analysis that the two preconditions for the four structural processes were consciously intended choices rather than unintended by-products. More specifically the new president of the firm and the corporate officers discussed and chose them deliberately. Hence assumptions or axioms that are set by the new president and the corporate officers play an important role in changing old and creating new cultural realities. They also influence the type of directory knowledge. Only an evolutionary perspective could reveal this information about the formation, change, and institutionalization of cultural knowledge. It also includes information about the role of a new president or leader in these processes.

The boundaries for cultural groupings in regard to axiomatic knowledge are located at the top management level. The negotiated personal beliefs and experiences of the new president and the corporate officers influenced the content of axiomatic knowledge. The grouping and the respective cultural knowledge are maintained and perpetuated through role modeling, mentorship, symbolic rewards, and control through selection.

Chapters 5 to 8 describe and discuss these findings further before I integrate them into an empirically based model of cultural knowledge. Chapter 9 integrates the major findings into a general framework of cultural knowledge in organizations, while Chapter 10 discusses some of the insights about cultural knowledge, strategy, and organizational processes. Chapter 11 draws conclusions on the nature and concept of culture in organizations. Chapter 12 indicates some of the study's implications for future research and for understanding cultural settings.

NOTES

1. Burns (1975).
2. Handy (1978).
3. Harrison (1972) was the first to propose the distinction among these four kinds of cultures.
4. Martin et al. (1983).

FIVE

Dictionary Knowledge: Cultural Groupings at the Descriptive Level

This chapter describes and discusses the findings regarding dictionary knowledge which was defined as commonly-held knowledge about definitions and descriptions. It refers to the "what is" in a given cultural setting. This chapter includes the nature, content, and structure of the dictionary themes as well as the location of cultural groupings. Throughout the text the firm is labeled BIND. The reader is reminded that the results are restricted to a case study of one firm $(N = 1)$[1] and that the information was obtained in regard to the firm's major innovations or changes as defined by its members. These two aspects limit the ability to generalize from the findings.[2]

Overall the results of the analysis of dictionary information can be summarized in five major points. The first one refers to the *nature* of dictionary knowledge, the second is a finding about *cultural groupings*. This last one is further specified in findings three, four, and five:

(1) Dictionary knowledge across respondents can be classified into four major themes. The first deals with the company's major *goal*

and its accomplishment. The second one refers to the aspect of *strategy*, both intended and realized. The third one is related to the *structure* of the company, and the fourth one relates to the *orientation toward organizational members*.

(2) Organizational members were found to form cultural groupings according to perceived functional domains. These groupings are encouraged, especially through rewards, incentives, and other organizational control systems.

(3) The nature of dictionary knowledge changes with hierarchic levels from a general nature, at the top, to increasing concreteness at lower levels in the company.

(4) Priorities and emphases in dictionary knowledge change across divisions in relation to the major concerns, goals, and identity of a division. Identity in this context refers to the division's major products and related procedures and skills.

(5) Incentives, rewards, and other organizational control systems may contribute to the formation of cultural groupings according to perceived functional domains. They also help maintain these cultural groupings according to perceived functional domains.

THEMES OF DICTIONARY KNOWLEDGE

Dictionary knowledge is defined as lexical information that refers to knowledge of things or events at a descriptive level. In this study it refers to various descriptions of innovations/changes. Each respondent was asked to name three innovations/changes that he or she considered to be the major ones of the company. In the analysis of the innovations that were mentioned by all interviewees, four basic themes and one rudimentary one emerged. Based on their content I labeled these themes *goal and accomplishments, strategy, structure, orientation toward organizational members,* and *physical work environment.*

These themes represent abstractions from the data. They have emerged in repeated processes of comparing and contrasting all information that was obtained regarding dictionary knowledge. The themes were then checked against the original interview data and labeled with a common denominator that reflects their underlying meaning. In addition the chosen label should make sense to managers and organizational theorists. The distinctions between themes is not as clear-cut as their labels may suggest. They are interrelated with each other and to some extent codefined. Strategy follows from but may also redefine goal and accomplishments. The chosen distinctions reflect the specific interpretations and emphases that members of the company made. They represent their core ideas and basic concerns. These themes appear useful both for describing the data and for a better understanding of the nature of dictionary knowledge.

Theme 1: Goal and Accomplishments

The theme *goal and accomplishments* refers to what people considered the major goal of their company. But it also includes the specific realizations of this goal in form of concrete accomplishments. This theme expresses the members' both past and current intention to head toward this ideal and to bring about the desired results. The ideal is, however, not a terminal end state. It has the quality of a process goal that can be approximated only in a continuous, unending effort. This theme also comprises specific examples that indicate that the goal has been and is being realized.

The goal of building a successful and stable company was considered a major innovation or change among interviewees. Twelve years prior to the study, the stock of the company had plummeted. Since that time they have achieved a major turnaround. Organizational members intended to make the company more successful under more stable conditions. Monetary performance measures show that the company has moved toward this goal over the past 10 years and that it still is. The company has grown and consolidated over the years both internally and externally. Concrete indicators are growing sales and return on equity, a growing number of successful divisions, a growing number of employees, expanding departments and machinery, facilities that run out of space, and increasing work loads.

These indicators not only were mentioned in the interviews as major innovations or changes that have occurred in the company, I could also observe them during my visits in the different locations. They all had the meaning of working toward or having accomplished the commonly held goal of building a stable and successful company.

Theme 2: Strategy

The theme *strategy* comprises innovations that show *how* the goal of building a successful and stable company has been and is being accomplished. This theme does not refer to the goal itself. Instead it expresses the means by which the goal is being attained. This theme also consists of an intended and realized aspect. "Controlled profitable growth" is the overarching intended strategy. It indicates how to make and keep the company successful and stable.

Externally, controlled profitable growth is realized by simultaneous contraction and expansion. The firm sells divisions that have been unprofitable over a period of three years and that are involved in business that is influenced by style or changes in taste, such as furniture, carpets, or boats. They realize expansion through controlled and careful acquisition of companies that have to fit both factual and nonfactual parameters. On the factual side a company needs to be in a business in which BIND sees its major future growth, and it should add to BIND's existing product lines. The less factual parameters refer to a certain type of management and a way of thinking that has to correspond to the way BIND's management thinks and acts.

Internally, controlled profitable growth can also be characterized by simultaneous contraction and expansion. It is realized in four different ways and reflected in work behaviors and in production, marketing, and sales strategies. The contraction side is expressed in work efficiency, while expansion is emphasized through profitable sales, the introduction of new products, and customer services. *Efficiency in work* refers both to saving time and resources in work processes and to maintaining product quality at a high level. Or, as one person expresses it, "producing fast without cheating the customer."

Profitable sales refers to a strategy of selling quality and services rather than price. People feel that more and better growth can be achieved by selling good products and services rather than by cutting prices to outmaneuver competitors. They interpret "more and better" growth in terms of long-term and stable growth. Bargaining over prices is considered more or less taboo. They believe that customers who are only concerned about the price are ultimately disloyal. They will negotiate if the deal is likely to win a new customer and if they regard it as the first step toward a long-term business relationship.

They consider the expansion of products or moving into different types of products as the major means to increase the company's market share, to win new customers, and hence to achieve controlled profitable growth. Here again they develop and promote those products that yield the highest profit margin, that are likely to have a long life cycle, and, therefore, that promise to be winners. They try to identify products that are necessary but that no other company wants to produce because they are either difficult to manufacture or are unpopular. Or they take on products that the customer can no longer produce in a profitable way. They extend the range of existing products by production procedures that were developed elsewhere. Or they start distributing new exclusive products. They expect that these products will expand their current customer base by adding new long-term and viable customers and hence become major contributors to the overall intended goal of building a successful and stable company.

They use their focus on the quality and expansion of their customer services to intensify relationships with existing customers to obtain more of their total orders. They constantly seek ways to better service their customers' existing needs, to expand the servicing of their customers' current needs, and to identify potential future needs. Customers are informed and educated about the company's products and skills; new products are tested for the customer; and telephone lines and people are added to immediately respond to a customer's needs and to deliver needed products—even on a Sunday. They form the kind of relationships with their customers that make their products and services irreplaceable. Services span from production and quality testing to distribution as well as servicing machinery. Employees undertake major efforts to help customers become winners and, in return, become winners themselves through controlled, profitable, and long-term growth.

Two themes operate as framing parameters for goal achievement and strategy realization. One refers to the company's structure and the other to its social relationships among organizational members. The two themes will be described next.

Theme 3: Structure

The theme *structure* refers to structural aspects and formal procedures of the company. These provide the conditions that enable the achievement of the major intended goal and the realization of the general strategy. This theme consists of dictionary information of innovations that refer to the corporate structure and the design of the company, including its management information systems, control systems, and human resource systems.

The interviewees consider the corporate structure itself to be a major innovation. The rules and procedures standardize administrative work and assist in day-to-day activities concerning finances, accounting, information, control, and human resource administration. The rationale behind the company's design is to centralize as little as necessary to become and stay a successful and stable company through controlled profitable growth.

The corporate office sees its major responsibilities as the best servicing of its divisions. They try to accomplish this by coaching, advising, and controlling and by integrating the activities of the different divisions. The corporate office acts as an umbrella to protect and further BIND's activities. People located at the corporate office assist the divisions in their production by taking care of some of the routine work. Monthly financial statements are consolidated and turned into annual reports by people at the corporate office, who also take care of tax matters. Physical expansion, reorganization, and real estate transactions for the relocation of facilities are handled by the corporate office. Human resource systems such as health insurance, fringe benefits, profit sharing plans, and, to some extent, incentive plans are provided through the corporate office. Legal and "head hunting" services are available, and reductions in division overhead costs are facilitated by controlling and updating communication systems that are of general interest to all divisions. Financial matters are handled by investment of surplus funds and by providing funds that are necessary for a division's investment to grow. This solvency, in turn, establishes the divisions' credibility among suppliers as well as among customers.

Control, coaching, and information flow are achieved through the "operations group" formed by the vice presidents and president. Each vice president is functionally responsible for several divisions that operate in industries that he knows and with which he has experience.[3] The respective vice presidents examine their monthly statements carefully. Each indicates areas for necessary and/or possible improvements. And each helps the general managers of the divisions explore and find ways to improve. Decisions that involve an investment of more than $5,000 have to be justified and "sold" to the vice president. He may then discuss the issues with the other officers before he approves or rejects them. Furthermore he acts as a consultant to the divisions by recommending certain procedures or by passing on information of interest. He may play the role of devil's advocate in decision processes to broaden perspectives and question approaches. And he serves as a link between divisions and top management by informing the other members of top management about issues at the divisional level.

Frequent informal discussions and regular weekly meetings between members of the operations group foster information flow and integration at the top management level. The BIND business system is used as a linkage between the divisions and the corporate office, between the divisions and suppliers, and between the divisions. It is a computer system that had been developed over the five years prior to the study to computerize accounting procedures and inventory management. Inventories are intended to be shared in the future among divisions, and the system is expected to improve customer services through faster availability and delivery of products.

The structure theme also contains a management information and production control system that is being developed and that is considered as a major—future—innovation at the PC division.

Theme 4: Orientation Toward Organizational Members

The theme *orientation toward organizational members* is the second framing parameter that enables BIND to achieve its overall intended goal and to realize its strategy of controlled profitable growth. Innovations that are considered to be major ones refer to BIND's people orientation. The theme comprises management's attitude toward and relations with employees. Their special orientation is expressed in formal human resource systems as well as informally in daily activities.

One aspect of the orientation toward organizational members theme is fair treatment of employees that is based on an implicit social contract of mutual exchange: "We will treat you fairly if you show commitment to us." Another aspect is independence and responsibility—the notion that the overall goal of building a successful and stable company can only be accomplished if everybody does his or her share.

The profit sharing plan is designed to encourage employees to identify with that company goal. In addition the company is willing to provide both security and opportunities to people. Management at all levels emphasizes long-term employment that is reflected in long tenure. Workers are cross-trained both to avoid layoffs in recessionary times and to increase their competence and skills. Employees are promoted from within whenever possible. They can move around within and between divisions to find the job they like best. The idea is to let them do what they do best, to provide incentives to encourage them to do their best, and to reward them for doing their best.

Management shows their recognition in various monetary and symbolic ways such as bonuses, improved health care and dental plans, increased employees' responsibilities, educational programs, Christmas parties, excursions to ball games and to Disneyland, or through some kind of "trophy." One of the staff members at the corporate office who had worked at BIND for one year when interviewed, and was familiar with a wide range of different companies due to his prior work, phrases this orientation toward people as follows:

> I don't want to say they are futuristic, but going along with the times. Most companies are very behind the times in their management styles. I think we are very progressive.

Theme 5: Physical Work Environment

The last theme is rather rudimentary and shows only traces in comparison with the other four themes. It represents another framing parameter for goal achievement and strategy realization. People express their concern about the physical work environment either in terms of avoiding any kind of "bottlenecks" or in terms of facilitating work processes. This theme has the quality of a hygiene factor for employees. The mentioned aspects do not seem to influence productivity directly.

They act as intervening variables in that they seem to have an effect on employees' satisfaction at work. Organizational members either like the physical work environment or they dislike it.[4]

To summarize, these themes—especially the four themes goal and accomplishment, strategy, structure, and orientation toward organizational members—reflect dictionary knowledge of what is considered to be major innovations and changes at BIND. This information does not reflect the totality of cultural knowledge that organizational members have available. Instead it focuses only on those aspects that are considered important and that are emphasized by organizational members. Future research is required to determine the extent to which these themes are generic to companies at large, which may shed further light on the themes' appropriateness and comprehensiveness in describing and clarifying the major emphases placed within and across organizations and industries.

So far I have only described these themes and explained their specific meanings within the cultural context of BIND. Little has been said about their structure. This structure is addressed and examined in the next section.

THE STRUCTURE OF DICTIONARY THEMES

All four themes that I identified in regard to dictionary knowledge have a specific structure in common. For each theme dictionary knowledge can be arranged along two co-varying dimensions. One dimension expresses the extent of concreteness ranging from a rather general idea to specific instances. The other dimension expresses the notion of intention and different degrees of realizing this intention.

From intention to realization. Each theme shows a level of intention and various levels of realization. Intentions—the most abstract level of a theme—express a desire or an ideal. Intentions are guiding parameters for actions. They represent the design and plan behind actions. Realized ideas are specific instances, concrete examples of the company's move toward this ideal. They express concrete actions that have been undertaken to materialize a specific intention.

While the intentions behind themes were predominantly found at the top management level and to some extent at the level of middle management, the realizations of themes could be found at all levels investigated in the company. Their extent of concreteness differed, however.

From general to specific. Each theme is illustrated by examples of different levels of concreteness that covary with hierarchic levels. The most general realization of an intended theme was found at the top management level. More specific illustrations of the themes were found at the level of middle management while the most specific examples and instances of themes were located at the lower levels of production and administration.

These different levels of realizations and concreteness are, however, not quite as clear-cut. They were found to overlap successively. While top management's dictionary knowledge dominated at the most general level of realization, it also contained examples at the next, more concrete or more specific level of theme realization.

The dictionary knowledge of middle management had an intermediate level of specificity. But middle management also showed knowledge of themes at the most specific level of realization and, in some instances, at the most general level. This successive overlap indicates a brokerage function of middle management. It links top management with lower levels in the company and vice versa. The resulting design is close to Likert's concept of overlapping groups.[5] The realization of intended themes at the top management level can become intentions for the management at the division level.

Lower in the hierarchy dictionary knowledge was concentrated at the most specific level. Employees gave the most concrete realizations of themes, often from a perspective of the perceived implications that they personally felt.

Each theme is now discussed from this structural perspective. The numbers in parentheses indicate how many interviewees mentioned a particular component of a theme.

Goal and Accomplishments

From intentions of success to growth as accomplishment and perceived implications. The various components of this theme are shown in Figure 5.1. At the level of intentions, their most general goal is to build a successful and stable company (4). They consider the growth of BIND—both internally as well as externally—as the most general indicator that this goal has been and is being realized (7). Yearly increases in sales volume (5) and a higher return on equity (4) are mentioned as more specific illustrations of the goal's accomplishment. Several interviewees mentioned the growth of the particular division as a major innovation (18). This growth as an accomplishment represents a more specific realization of the overall goal or intention for BIND. People mentioned constant improvements (6) as manifestations of building a successful and stable company.

Interviewees gave a large number of specific examples that indicate the most concrete realizations and impacts. They may also refer to effects of the intended goal of building a successful and stable company and its realization in terms of company growth. More employees have been hired over the past years (8). For some people this growth implies job security (5), while for others the increasing work load is prevalent (2). Other manifestations of this growth are an expanded inspection department (3), decreasing physical space (3), more vehicles for deliveries (3), the opening of a small subsidiary (2), a faster work pace (2), and a change in work force composition (1).

Examples at the most concrete level of realization were predominantly given by organizational members at lower levels. These examples reflect perceived changes rather than innovations that have taken place over the past years. Because the term *innovation* was too abstract for lower-level employees,

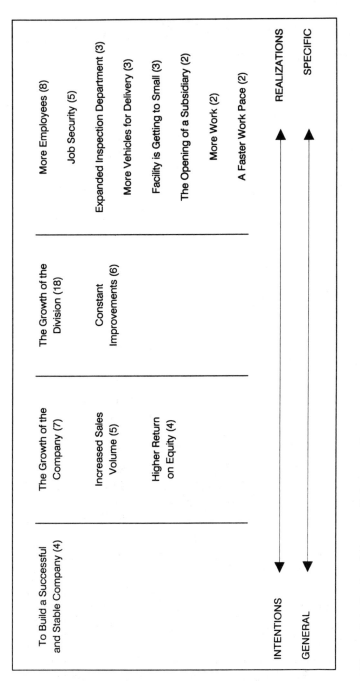

Figure 5.1. Goal and Accomplishments: From Intentions of Success to Growth as Accomplishments and Perceived Implications

Note: ( ) = Number of respondents who mentioned this particular issue

it was further specified as "changes that have taken place over the past years—changes that made things different than before."

Strategy

Finding a niche and maintaining and expanding it. The various components of this theme are listed in Figure 5.2. The general intention of this theme is captured in identifying a niche and keeping and expanding it through controlled profitable growth. At the most general level of realization, two illustrations are given: external growth by acquisition (1) and internal growth by profitable sales (8) and customer service (7).

More elaborate and concrete examples of how controlled profitable growth is being achieved internally were found at lower levels. These manifestations of the theme refer to the production strategy (13), to the marketing (3) and to the sales strategy (8) as well as to changes in general management (5).

Interviewees gave five specific examples of innovations related to the production strategy. Their production strategy is geared to realize the division's growth by making it "unique." People considered the introduction of new machines based on new technology an important innovation (13). They also considered the production of more complex parts (6) as well as of new and different parts (5) as innovative because the related profit margins are higher. Three people mentioned an emphasis on quality control (3). This was, however, associated with a negative change (2) due to some problems that had occurred a year earlier.

The marketing strategy is characterized by an orientation toward growth and the identification of a niche (4). Specific examples are keeping the customer informed (6), educating the customer about what the company can do for him or her (12), nourishing customer relations (3), and specializing distribution (1).

Most illustrations of the sales strategy can be and were summarized in the GA division with the concept of "offering the

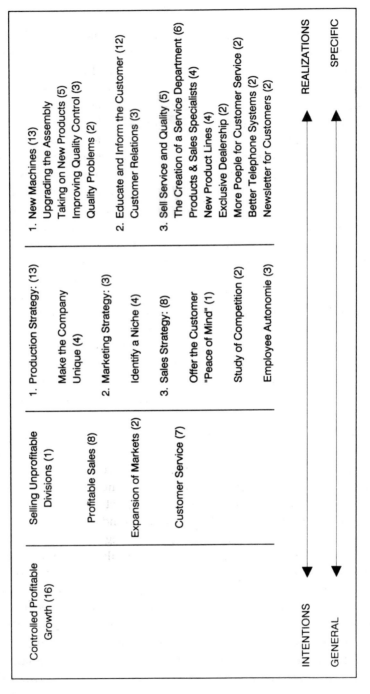

Controlled Profitable Growth (16)	Selling Unprofitable Divisions (1)	1. Production Strategy: (13)	1. New Machines (13)
			Upgrading the Assembly
	Profitable Sales (8)	Make the Company Unique (4)	Taking on New Products (5)
			Improving Quality Control (3)
			Quality Problems (2)
	Expansion of Markets (2)	2. Marketing Strategy: (3)	2. Educate and Inform the Customer (12)
		Identify a Niche (4)	Customer Relations (3)
	Customer Service (7)	3. Sales Strategy: (8)	3. Sell Service and Quality (5)
		Offer the Customer "Peace of Mind" (1)	The Creation of a Service Department (6)
			Products & Sales Specialists (4)
		Study of Competition (2)	New Product Lines (4)
			Exclusive Dealership (2)
		Employee Autonomie (3)	More People for Customer Service (2)
			Better Telephone Systems (2)
			Newsletter for Customers (2)

INTENTIONS   REALIZATIONS

GENERAL   SPECIFIC

Figure 5.2 Strategy: Finding a Niche, Maintaining and Expanding It

customer peace of mind." Selling service instead of price (5) is one important specification of this theme. Further specifications are the development and expansion of an equipment service department (6), the distribution of new product lines (4), the development of sales and production specialists (4), exclusive dealerships (2), same day and emergency delivery (2), an increased number of employees to service customers (3), a newsletter that informs customers about changes in the industry and the company's services (2), a new telephone system with an increased number of lines to help avoid placing a customer on hold (2).

Five interviewees considered a change in general management a major innovation (5). They specified that the new general manager furthered the growth of the division by reinvesting in it (2) rather than taking out all the surplus. In addition he encouraged study of the competition on an ongoing basis (2) and gave his employees flexibility in actions (2). In the other division, however, the general manager was considered by two people to be a potential impediment to realization of the intended strategy and to accomplishment of the intended goal of future growth.

Structure

Corporate structure and its implications. The components of this theme are listed in Figure 5.3. At its most general level structure as major innovation means the corporate structure or the design of BIND (4). This was and still is intended to provide the most appropriate conditions for conducting BIND's business. *Appropriate* is interpreted as adjusting simultaneously to internal as well as to external conditions.

Realization of the corporate structure at the most general level is demonstrated in the formation and existence of the operations group (2). This is composed of the president and vice presidents. Two people mentioned centralized finances and standardized accounting procedures (2), human resource systems (5), the BIND business computer system (9), and the

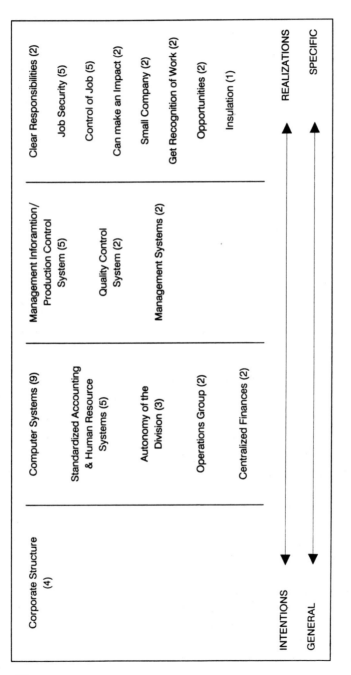

Corporate Structure (4)	Computer Systems (9)	Management Inforamtion/ Production Control System (5)	Clear Responsibilities (2)
	Standardized Accounting & Human Resource Systems (5)	Quality Control System (2)	Job Security (5)
			Control of Job (5)
	Autonomy of the Division (3)		Can make an Impact (2)
		Management Systems (2)	Small Company (2)
	Operations Group (2)		Get Recognition of Work (2)
	Centralized Finances (2)		Opportunities (2)
			Insulation (1)

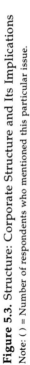

INTENTIONS   REALIZATIONS

GENERAL   SPECIFIC

Figure 5.3. Structure: Corporate Structure and Its Implications
Note: ( ) = Number of respondents who mentioned this particular issue.

autonomy of divisions in finding their own means of best accomplishing the intended and agreed upon goals (3).

In general, in the development of BIND's structure, the guiding parameters were to create as little centralization as necessary and to provide as much divisional autonomy as possible. People at the corporate office saw their collective responsibility as enabling the divisions' autonomy by providing centralized administrative services. These also serve as integrators. Hence divisions have to follow the accounting guidelines set by top management, their financial policies, and their human resource policies and services.

At the next level the theme structure is realized in management systems (3), in a management information and production control system (2), and in a quality control system (2). The latter two were still in the process of being developed at the time of the study. Some interviewees mentioned, as innovations that have to occur in the near future, the management information system (8) and the production control system (2).

At the most concrete level of realization, the theme structure is interpreted and perceived as clear responsibilities (2), as being in control of the job (2), as the ability to make an impact (2) and get recognition for one's work (2), as providing opportunities for different kind of jobs (2), and in terms of a "small" company. Employees interpret smallness as a positive factor in regard to job security, opportunities, and interpersonal relations.

A potentially negative side of the divisional autonomy lies in its tendency to isolate (1) and in the feeling of not knowing exactly what goes on in the rest of the company. As one employee expresses it:

> Here at BIND [in comparison with another company] everything is so secretive. You don't really know what's happening other than outside your building. You feel like nothing else exists, and anything you really understand about BIND is confined to your building. Basically you don't come in contact with a lot of people. You feel very neglected.

Orientation Toward Organizational Members

A bias toward people and its manifestations. Figure 5.4 lists the various components of this theme. The theme orientation toward organizational members is most generally intended as a *people orientation*. It can be characterized as fair treatment of people—both intended and perceived—in terms of providing opportunities (6), responsibility (6), and various human resource systems.

At the next level the theme is further specified as "good (people-oriented) management." Interviewees perceived and characterized it as being fair and supportive (16) and being given chances (5), promotion from within (5), incentive plans (4), the company's profit sharing plan (4), and opportunities given to organizational members to let them do what they do best (2).

At the most specific level of realization, the management aspect of the theme is further illustrated by descriptions such as listening (7), encouraging (6), supporting and trusting (5), instilling confidence (4), helping people progress (2), and partnership (1). Interviewees characterized relationships among people as good (12) in a relaxed atmosphere (6). One employee's description:

> And I think that's an innovative thing in the company that most companies don't have. They put confidence in you. You show them your ability, they will instill confidence in you and allow you to do your thing as long as you continue to succeed. If you'd screw up, you'd hear about it. You'd sit down and talk about it.

Fair treatment of people is further specified as having opportunities (6), no layoffs (2), good benefits (7), good health (1) and dental insurance (2), and good pay (1). One employee describes this in more detail:

> He [the general manager] treats everybody very, very nice, very fairly, *very* fairly. If you have a problem, regardless if it's personal which is not always good to take a personal

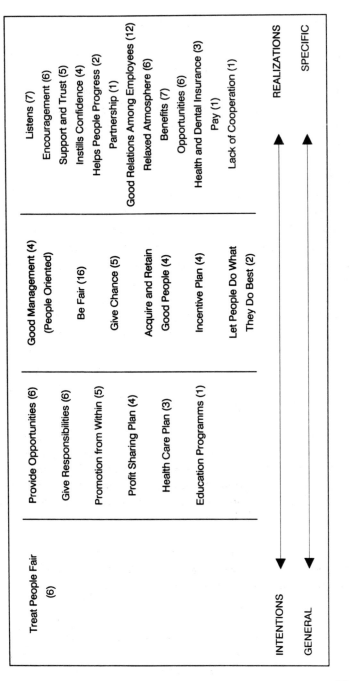

Figure 5.4. Orientation Toward People: A Bias Toward People and Its Manifestations

Note: ( ) = Number of respondents who mentioned this particular issue.

problem to management, but if it becomes that you need time off or whatever, he listens and doesn't judge. So he's very fair and I'd say that the majority here feels that way. Very down to earth and very *easy* to work with.

Three people mentioned negative aspects. They concern management, a lack of cooperation, and the cancellation aspect of the profit sharing plan. All three people were lower-level employees. The person who did not like management was also dissatisfied with his type of work, and he was to leave the company for a completely different job. The person dissatisfied with the profit sharing plan had taken a loan from it. He felt punished because part of the money contributed by the company was taken out upon his withdrawal, as specified in the policy. The last example for a negative innovation or change was given by a person who was relatively new to BIND. Based on her prior work experience, she felt that people were not very cooperative at work. This problem was being interpreted by middle management as a lack of communication. This constitutes, however, a symptom rather than the cause. The lack of cooperation as perceived seems to be predominantly due to the special kind of incentive system that existed in this division. This incentive system will be described in more detail below.

Physical Work Environment

Facilitation or burden. An additional—more rudimentary—theme surfaced from the data in regard to the work environment. At the most general level the physical work environment is a factor that may facilitate or hinder conducting business. A general guideline in space planning and interior design is, for example, the avoidance of bottlenecks (1). At a more concrete level of realization, the physical design of the division is considered to facilitate work (2). At the most concrete level the physical work environment is perceived as either pleasant (4) or unpleasant (6) depending on the specific workplace of an individual.

In the previous two sections I have described and explicated the content and structure of the themes in regard to dictionary knowledge. No link has yet been made to the specific locations of each theme and their various realizations. Such a link reveals cultural groupings that I describe in the following section.

CULTURAL GROUPINGS

An analysis of the specific location of each theme and its various illustrations shows that all themes are present in each of the three different research sites within BIND. Differences exist, however, both within and across divisions in how priorities are set. The researched divisions emphasized the various themes differently. Emphasis was determined as a combination of the frequency of mention and the extent of description. More specifically I found the following:

(1) The emphasis placed on each theme varies according to functional domain and according to a division's identity. *Functional domain* is defined as the totality of functions for which people consider themselves to be responsible. *Divisional identity* refers to what is considered the major product of the division as well as product-related procedures, skills, or technology.

(2) The boundaries and interpretations of cultural groupings according to perceived functional domain are associated with the level of analysis. More specifically I could make the following observations regarding cultural groupings as defined:

(a) At the divisional level of analysis, cultural groupings tend to form according to functional domains within and across divisional boundaries. The perceived functions of each domain influence its interpretations.

(b) At the company's level of analysis I also found cultural groupings to form according to perceived functional domains. Their boundaries and interpretations are, however, influenced by a division's identity.

(c) The formation of cultural groupings according to functional domains is closely related to incentive and reward systems. Aspects of organizational design and other control systems help maintain this formation of cultural groupings.

These findings are supported by data at the directory level of knowledge. I will further illustrate them below. Given the inductive paradigm of the research project, these results are in the nature of hypotheses. They need further testing in subsequent research efforts.

I found the following cultural groupings in the three divisions of BIND:

- a design and control grouping
- a production grouping (composed of several groupings identified in a finer-grained analysis)
- a managerial marketing or managerial sales grouping
- a coordination grouping

The design and control grouping is located at the corporate office. Production, managerial marketing, and coordination groupings are located at the PC division, and the managerial sales grouping was identified in the GA division. Based on a preliminary analysis of data collected at the PC division, the hypothesis emerged that cultural groupings form according to perceived functional domains. I examined this hypothesis further by collecting and analyzing data from sales people at the GA division. The results of this analysis support and further specify the hypothesis.

Sales people in the GA division form a grouping similar to the grouping in the PC division. The emphases placed in these two groupings differ, however, in regard to the groups' specific interpretation of their respective functional domains. These differences in interpretation seem to be due to their different divisional identities. Organizational members in the two divisions identified with different industries and compared themselves with companies with a different business nature. PC is manufacturing oriented and GA is distribution oriented. The focus of the sales people in the manufacturing division is more marketing oriented whereas the focus of the distribution division's sales people is predominantly sales and services oriented.

I describe and discuss each one of the identified groupings in the following section.

Design and Control Grouping

At the corporate headquarters, the so-called operations group forms a cultural grouping that is more appropriately characterized as a design and control grouping. It consists of the president and vice presidents. All members of this group were interviewed except the Northern California regional executive.

This group places major emphasis on the intended aspect of themes and their most general level of realization. The members of this grouping create, develop, and design those aspects that should be focused on and emphasized in running the company and its various divisions. The members of this group are most interested in building and maintaining a successful and stable company through internal and external growth rather than being occupied with the concrete aspects of how this is achieved. They want to see realized their designed and intended strategy of controlled profitable sales. With their emphasis on profitable sales, on product quality, and on consumer service, they leave up to the division's management the way to realize controlled, profitable growth.

The design and control grouping exerts various means of control to ensure that the divisions do grow in a controlled and profitable fashion. Each division is responsible to one of the vice presidents. Division managers have to justify their monthly balance sheets, their expenses, and their future investments to their designated vice president. He sets goals jointly with them for the division. He points out areas for necessary improvements. And he may give a set of recommendations to them about what can be done to further improve.

Successes are shared with the general managers in form of bonuses, profit sharing plans, and stock options. In addition they express their recognition with trophies for the most profitable division, for the division with the highest profitable growth, and other company targets. The winning general managers receive these trophies at their annual meeting in a resort area.

Production Groupings

I identified a production grouping in the PC division that consists of people involved in various aspects of the production cycle. Their dictionary knowledge had the most specific nature. Concrete illustrations of themes were predominantly related to immediate work experiences. This "localism" is the most prominent factor that differentiates this grouping from others. Another differentiating aspect is the importance of the physical work environment. Each member of this grouping mentioned aspects of the physical work environment whereas only two other respondents in two different cultural groupings referred to it.

A finer-grained analysis of this production grouping revealed that it is composed of several groupings. These groupings relate to a more specified differentiation into functional domains. Innovations or changes named as the major ones by workers in the electronic subsystems were different than those named by workers on the shop floor, regardless of the department in which they were working, and those named by the inspectors. The nature of work, and hence the interpretation of their respective functional domains, seems to have a major influence on the formation of these three groupings.

Electronics. Workers in the electronic subsystems (3) most often mentioned aspects of the physical work environment. They generally had difficulties in thinking of major changes because they had produced the same parts for 20 years. Even if some of the parts changed, the work process remained basically the same. They all liked their work conditions and characterized them as nice as well as clean, with a large work space, with the possibility of having "intelligent" discussions while working, and the small size of the unit, which they associated with job security. Even if they considered their work to be routine, they felt that it required more intelligence than working on the shop floor. The members of this grouping made a clear distinction in regard to inclusion and exclusion, between "we" and "them." Shop-floor workers were referred to as "push-buttons." They had adopted this expression from one of the engineers.

The electronic subsystems is located adjacent to the shop floor. The nature of the work requires air-conditioning and cleanliness. Walking through the doors from the shop floor felt like entering a different world. It was much more quiet, clean, bright, and spacious.

Shop-floor production. People working on the shop floor (5) mentioned concrete illustrations of all five themes. Most prevalent were, however, those aspects that referred to the division's growth and the physical work environment. The members of this group gave specific examples for the division's growth in terms of an increasing number of employees, constant improvements, decreasing work space, and job security. But they also included a fast work pace that was considered too fast by one of the respondents. They interpreted the introduction of new machines and new parts for production in terms of a strategy change.

The theme of orientation toward people was expressed in terms of good benefits, good insurance plans, cross-training, and no layoffs. They felt that communications had improved since "one of them" had become plant supervisor. He was a Spanish-speaking, trained engineer who had started to work in the PC division as a machine operator before he transferred to engineering. Despite his training he came back to the shop floor because he preferred this type of work.

Each shop-floor worker who was interviewed complained about the physical work environment. They described it as too dirty, too hot, and too small. One person blamed the lack of cleanliness on the janitor, while others felt that it was general management, which was criticized as not reinvesting sufficiently into the plant.

Inspection. The "inspection" grouping differs from the other two groupings in that its members identify with and frequently refer to the professional training they acquired prior to joining the PC division. They interpret, for example, the introduction of a coordinate measurement machine not only in terms of helping them in their work but also in terms of helping them to learn new skills.

The nature of their work requires both a higher skill level and more knowledge as compared with the other two production groupings. Inspectors have to be licensed by the state and must pass an examination. These procedures, which may have the nature of rites of passage, are likely to foster professional identification.[6] In addition they felt that the nature of their work required taking the customers' rather than the company's perspective. This may be another factor of their professional focus and identity.

Part of this professional identity may also be due to the fact that three of the five inspectors had worked at PC for three months or less. They had worked as inspectors before and felt that there were only a few specifics that they had to learn at PC in addition to their existing knowledge. Identification with their professional role still seemed to be stronger than their identification with the company or division.[7]

The physical work environment was important to this grouping in that they liked their clean, air-conditioned room, which they contrasted with the dirty, hot, and noisy shop floor. This clean, officelike environment may be an additional factor for their closer association with management than with people on the shop floor.

Managerial Marketing Grouping

The managerial marketing grouping at PC consists of the division's sales people. Their major focus is on realization of the themes *goal and accomplishments* and *strategy* by making the division successful through profitable growth. The members of this grouping are more concerned with marketing than with selling the division's products. These are considered to "sell themselves." Their marketing strategy is geared toward expanding their current market share by acquiring new customers as well as by increasing their orders from existing customers. They intend to achieve the latter through a change in production strategy and using already established relationships with customers. The members of this group try to identify new and more profitable parts for production. In addition they attempt to produce more complex parts by drawing on various skills on the shop floor and in the electronics assembly. They then inform and educate existing customers about the capacities available at PC to produce needed products.

The members of the managerial marketing grouping exhibit a strong entrepreneurial—or rather intrapreneurial—nature that is supported by the division's reward structure. All sales people are fully commissioned without having a company expense account. They are, in many ways, self-employed, without most of the responsibilities that go with it. One of them expresses this as follows: "There are no limits to your earnings and you don't have to meet a payroll, but it makes you worry about the future of the company."

All of them were full about ideas how to make the company—hence their income—grow. They combined their ideas with a long-term perspective in terms of keeping existing customers satisfied, writing more orders, and winning new customers.

Coordination Grouping

At PC I identified a coordination grouping. This grouping links production groupings with the managerial marketing grouping. Thus the external focus of the managerial marketing grouping is combined with the internal focus of the production groupings. The coordination grouping has a more flexible and shifting membership in comparison with the other groupings. Membership composition shifts depending on the problems at hand. This fact gives it the nature of an institutionalized ad hoc group.

At its core is the general manager. Other members are one or both production control people, the sales person who represents the product in question, one of the engineers, the plant manager and/or the plant supervisor, the inspection control and electronic subsystems manager, and, at times, the controller and the vice president responsible for the PC division. Most of the core members hold managerial positions that determine the grouping's functional focus.

The foci of this coordination grouping may vary from general planning and decision making to problem solving. The members of the coordination grouping may discuss a decision about a major investment or they may meet to deal with a certain delivery deadline and its consequences. This grouping helps integrate different emphases and concerns within the division. It facilitates information exchange within the division as well as between divisions and top management.

The cultural groupings described above were identified within divisional boundaries. To further investigate and validate the hypothesis that had emerged about the formation of cultural groupings according to functional domains, I chose a third research site. I studied a division that had belonged to BIND for about the same length of time as the PC division in the last phase of data collection. The choice of the GA division was based upon considerations of factors that may jeopardize internal and external validity.[8] I considered the time factor most crucial because it influences the amount of cultural knowledge that develops. Several years may be needed to adopt or integrate cultural aspects after merging with or acquiring a company. The two divisions had been with BIND for 16 and 19 years, respectively. These time spans are comparable and sufficiently long for new cultural aspects to be adopted and old ones to be neutralized or integrated with the new ones.

In this last phase of data collection in the GA division, I selected respondents randomly from managerial positions and from the marketing and sales area. The random sampling strategy was thus complemented with purposive sampling to further investigate the hypothesis that cultural groupings form according to functional domains.

I conducted 12 interviews in the GA division. The analysis and interpretation of the resulting data support the hypothesis. GA sales people showed similar concerns about building a stable and successful company. They also used the same strategy to accomplish this goal: increasing the division's market share through controlled profitable growth.

Within this grouping I observed a shift in focus between the sales people in managerial positions—or senior sales people— and the junior sales people. The 5 senior sales people had worked for the GA division for a period of 8 to 24 years while the 17 juniors had started work within the last 5 years. Their hiring was due to the growth of the division, which began after the current general manager had joined the division.

The sales managers create new opportunities for sales. They try to get exclusive dealerships. They test promising new products with their customers. They find opportunities for technical training conducted by suppliers, and they conduct weekly educational sales meetings for junior sales people. The juniors rely on the seniors' knowledge and experience. They implement the strategies and programs designed by the sales managers.

Due to the division's identity in terms of major product and related procedures and skills, I found that the emphasis of the two divisions differed. While both divisions can be classified as service industries, they differ in the nature of their services. The GA division distributes and increasingly services graphic arts-related equipment and supplies. In contrast the PC division produces metal and electronic parts according to customer specifications. The market of the GA division is saturated to an extent that increasing its market share implies taking desirable business away from other major distributors. The sales people at PC feel, in contrast, that their division can still expand by securing orders that other—larger—manufacturers would not consider desirable. In addition the PC division identifies with manufacturing and compares itself with other manufacturing companies rather than with distribution companies.

These differences make the managerial sales grouping at GA predominantly concerned about aspects of selling rather than marketing. They try to find and develop different and better ways of selling. They attempt to increase their division's market share by getting exclusive dealerships and by finding creative ways to improve and add to their existing customer services. Their motto is to provide their customers with "peace of mind."

These findings support the notion that cultural groupings form according to functional domain defined by its members' perceived functions or responsibilities. But the findings also indicate that the same functional domains may be enacted differently by different divisions of the same company or different companies.

At the company's—rather than the division's—level of analysis, cultural groupings still seem to form according to functional domains. These functional domains are, however, influenced in their enactment by the division's—rather than the departments'—identity. This division identity is defined in terms of its major product and product-related procedures, skills, or technology. The results of this study propose at the company's level of analysis that the boundaries of cultural groupings according to functional domains are influenced by a division's identity and that similarities across different divisions are greater than across different functional domains within one division. This proposition needs to be tested with a larger sample of similar functional groupings pertaining to different companies. Another interesting hypothesis to investigate in future research is whether similarities between the same functional groupings across companies are larger than between different functional groupings within the same company.

Role of Rewards and Control Systems

Further analysis of the data suggests that the formation of cultural groupings according to perceived functional domains is closely related to existing incentive systems, reward systems, and control systems in general. Incentives and rewards support and may have contributed to the formation of cultural groupings according to functional domains. Aspects of organizational design such as formal control systems in the form of accounting procedures help maintain this formation of cultural groupings. Based on these insights, a new method to identify employees' membership in cultural groupings may be applied. One could ask organizational members, for example, to describe the kinds of behaviors or activities for which they are rewarded.[9]

Reward systems at BIND are designed so that organizational members are rewarded for the functions they are intended and supposed to perform and so that they identify with the company's major goal and strategies. Rewards exist for expected—that is, desired—behaviors. And controls exist for undesired performances. Based on the collected data, reward and control systems are congruent with functional domains and with organizational goals. They tend to focus on exceptions rather than rules and procedures. One employee explains:

> If you screwed up, you'd hear about it. Someone would talk to you, . . . we would have an open discussion. But as long as you are doing well and getting good results, there is no interference, you are allowed to go. I think that's amazing. I don't know if you can relate to that or not, but to me it's fascinating. No company is just like that.

Members of the *design and control grouping* are major individual shareholders of BIND's stock. They have a vested interest in the company's future performance. In addition to this monetary incentive, they also derive a large part of their identity from the company. Four of them had created, developed, and built one of BIND's divisions and had been with BIND as a company for as long as 34 years. Six of the eight members of this grouping worked together to create and set in place the company's overall design and to make it work. This large investment in terms of time, energy, and identity has created commitment to the company. This commitment represents not merely their financial security but also a strong means of personal identification. Half of their lives had been dedicated to the creation and maintenance of BIND.

The members of the *shop-floor and electronics production groupings* receive wages that they can increase substantially through a special kind of incentive system. It is based on the principle of producing quality parts fast. After having been employed at BIND for six months, they are eligible to participate in a profit sharing plan that is designed to make them identify with the company's intended process goal and its strategy of controlled profitable growth. The resulting growth and success of the company makes them proud of being a part of this success. In addition it gives them a means of personal identification. As one employee explains:

> Improving the company, I think that's very satisfying. You know you are part of the improvement of the company. To me that's real satisfying. You know, you spend eight hours (ten at PC) on the job, you better enjoy it. Otherwise, there is a lot of jobs out there. You gonna get another one.

The introduction of the incentive plan at other manufacturing divisions has shown subsequent increases in production of 20%. One drawback of this incentive system is its immediate focus on individual performance. In the PC division this has created a problem that is characterized as a communication problem, which was mentioned above. Workers are busy producing their parts and thinking of ways to cut time and procedures. These efforts distract them from thinking about possibilities for improving a part's preparation for the next step in the production cycle while they perform their own functions. What matters to them is the immediate work process for which they are held responsible on a route sheet. Even though the costs for rework or rejected parts are subtracted from their bonuses, they focus only on developing more efficient procedures for their immediate workstations. One of the employees who had worked at PC for only three weeks and who had a different experience at her prior workplace described this problem as follows:

> People don't seem to care here, only what they do. They don't care what's going on in the next job and what they have to do to make the next job easier. If I can make it easier on my part I do it. But a lot of people don't. They think "well, the next guy will take care of that." At the drill department, for example, changing the drill [would be easy, but] then they let it go. And in the burring department it's harder on them because they got too much burring to do. If they would change the drill, it would be a lot easier. They don't think this way, they just care about what they do, let the other department take care of that. I don't work like that.

The *managerial marketing group* is fully commissioned. They receive a percentage of profits rather than sales, which draws their attention to increasing profitable sales. Rather than just increasing sales, they focus on establishing long-term relationships to maintain and increase their income. This type of reward structure makes all of them think in entrepreneurial and managerial terms with a major focus on the relevant external environment. This external focus differentiates them from the other functional groupings.

The *coordination grouping* acts as a linkage or boundary spanner between the internal focus of production, the external focus of marketing, and the financial focus of the corporation. Its core member, the general manager, is salaried. He receives a yearly management bonus based on the performance of the division. He also has stock option privileges like all key employees. The department managers have similar privileges. Making the division perform successfully depends on their efforts to achieve integration among the various parts of the division. They also know about the unspoken rule that divisions are sold when they have been unprofitable for a period of three consecutive years. According to one verbal account, this rule had been applied about 25 times in the 14 years prior to the study.

These examples demonstrate that rewards, incentive, and control systems are closely related to the formation of cultural groupings according to functional domains. The question emerges at this point as to what kind of cultural groupings are likely to form if perceived functional responsibilities are not congruent with reward, incentive, and control systems. A guess would be that internal politics would play a more dominant role in the formation of cultural groupings. Such political behaviors were not observed in this company during the course of the study. This question needs to be addressed in subsequent research efforts.

SUMMARY

This chapter described and discussed the results and insights in regard to dictionary knowledge. Four major themes and one rudimentary one have been identified in the analysis of dictionary knowledge. I observed these themes in all three research sites within the same company. Due to their nature I have labeled them goal and accomplishments, strategy, structure, orientation toward organizational members, and physical work environment. Furthermore these themes tend to vary with hierarchy in their orientation and in their degree of specificity. I found a general design orientation at higher levels whereas an execution orientation with specific illustrations of the themes was observed at lower levels in the company. Middle management performed a brokerage function in mediating between the top and lower levels.

Cultural groupings emerged with boundaries forming according to functional domains. While all four themes were present across the identified cultural groupings, their emphasis varied from grouping to grouping at the organizational and at the divisional levels of analysis. Similarities seem to be larger between equivalent functional domains across divisions than between different functional domains within divisions. Incentives, rewards, organizational design, and other organizational control mechanisms tend to support this kind of cultural grouping according to functional domains. The next chapter discusses the findings in regard to directory knowledge.

NOTES

1. N = 1 refers to the organizational level of analysis. At the divisional level, it was n = 3. One may argue that three different companies were studied because the three divisions identify with different industries, but they are all part of the same organization.

2. Future research needs to determine the extent to which the findings of this case study can be replicated and generalized across organizations and across other issues that may be used to elicit cognitive components of culture.

3. The president as well as all of the vice presidents and the general managers are males. The use of *he* is, therefore, appropriate.

4. This finding is similar to Herzberg's (1966) research, in which he differentiates between motivators and hygiene factors.

5. The concept of overlapping groups is described in Likert (1967).

6. The ritualistic character of hiring and qualification procedures is discussed in Trice, Belasco, and Allutto (1969).

7. Identification with one's profession was found to increase with increasing levels of professional training (i.e., Gregory, 1983).

8. Campbell and Stanley (1974) discuss the problems of internal and external validity.

9. This strong influence of incentive and reward systems may be due to enveloping cultural aspects pertaining to U.S. society. In a discussion with a European scholar, a similarly strong influence of incentives and rewards was questioned within European companies.

SIX

Directory Knowledge: Cultural Synergism at the Process Level

This chapter presents findings from the analysis of directory knowledge which was defined as commonly-held knowledge about cause-and-effect relationships. This knowledge refers to processes and delineates the "how to" of things and events. More specifically this chapter discusses the content and nature of themes that have emerged at this level of analysis and describe the parameters that seem to be preconditions for the existence and enactment of the themes.

In the analysis of directory information, four themes have emerged across respondents—regardless of their position or function in the company. Even if the interviewees named and described completely different innovations, the process of how they came about showed the same underlying characteristics. Analysis of data obtained in regard to directory knowledge revealed *cultural synergism* rather than cultural groupings. In addition four common themes emerged that underlie the processes of achieving innovations and change at BIND. These themes refer to *the way tasks are accomplished, the way people relate to each other, the way adaptation or change is accomplished,* and *the acquisition and perpetuation of knowledge.* Two parameters seem to establish and create the conditions for these processes to happen. They are the organizational design of the company and the type of people working at BIND. The following part describes and analyzes cultural synergism, the four themes, and the two preconditions.

THE NATURE AND THE ANALYSIS OF DIRECTORY INFORMATION

Directory knowledge has been defined as process knowledge. It is operational knowledge, knowledge about causal-analytical relationships. It refers to the aspect of *how*—how, for example, specific innovations and changes come about. As such directory knowledge represents theories of action held by organizational members.

After the interviewees had named the three innovations or changes that they considered to be the major ones in the company and explained why, I asked them how each one of the innovations had come about. This exploration included the context in which each of them occurred, the people who were involved in initiating and carrying it through, where it happened, what kind of forces helped progressing, and which aspects hindered. I processed the interview data in four steps: First I analyzed each one of the mentioned innovations according to these aspects. In the second step of analysis, I compared and contrasted the resulting information across the three innovations that were given by an individual (individual analysis). And in a third step this "individual" information was compared and contrasted across respondents (group analysis). To determine the validity of these results, they were then compared with observational, demographic, and documentary data and checked against the original interview information.

Even if interviewees referred to completely different innovations that involved different types of activities, the analysis revealed that the underlying processes by which these different innovations were achieved are similar. It also did not matter whether the interviewees belonged to different cultural groupings in regard to dictionary knowledge. Despite their membership in different cultural groupings, no major differences emerged at the operational level across interviewees in how these processes were achieved. The few variations in interpretations and specific enactments only surfaced between divisions. These variations can be attributed to differences in the divisions' *identities*, which is defined in terms of the major products and related procedures, skills, or technology that pertain to the specific industry in which a division is involved.

Due to its nature I labeled this generic congruence in processes across respondents *cultural synergism*, a term which expresses the notion that organizational members seem to act independently of each other, yet the underlying processes in their actions are very similar. These processes are described and explained in the following section. Based on their predominant content and implied meanings, I labeled them *task accomplishment, relationships among people, adaptation and change,* and *acquisition and perpetuation of knowledge.*

These themes pertaining to directory knowledge are also interrelated and to some extent codefined. They constitute the areas on which strongest emphasis is placed in the company, and they were found most useful in characterizing and describing the obtained directory information. Future research needs to determine to what extent they are generic across organizations and whether they are comprehensive in describing and characterizing directory knowledge across organizations and industries.

PROCESS 1: TASK ACCOMPLISHMENT

This theme refers to the processes by which organizational members accomplish tasks. The interviewees mentioned several guidelines for behavior that relate to this theme, such as

"think of ways to save money"
"be efficient in what you do"

"see that everything gets done"
"get involved"
"take initiative"
"take responsibility"
"make an impact"
"rather make a wrong decision than no decision"
"stay informed"
"help each other out"
"we are in business together"

There are two major components to this theme. Based on their nature I labeled one *autonomy* and the other *team effort.* *Autonomy* refers to each individual's effort and dedicated contribution, whereas *team effort* portrays the coordination and integration of these individual efforts and contributions. Both are characterized by a certain way of behaving that can best be described as efficient and work oriented.

Autonomy

"Take initiative and see that everything gets done." In each of the three divisions, much emphasis is placed on people's individual—unique—contributions. Organizational members are expected to make useful contributions that, in turn, are considered by them to be major innovations/changes within the company. Of all the interviewees 29 named and described at least one innovation/change that they themselves believed they had initiated. They did not refer to their contributions in order to show off, neither did they mention that it was expected of them. Instead they considered it the "normal" and appreciated way of behaving at work within BIND. And they expressed pride in the fact that their input counts and that they can make an impact.

People with knowledge about and experience from other companies or those who had recently joined BIND emphasized this autonomy as something very special that they had learned to value. As one person expressed it:

As long as you are doing well and getting good results, there is no interference, you are allowed to go. I think that's amazing, I don't know if you can relate to that or not, but to me it's fascinating. No company is just like that.

Two other people who had recently joined different divisions at BIND made similar statements. This opportunity to make suggestions, to contribute, and to excel was a major difference to them.

One shop-floor worker at PC recalled, as an another example, that he did not want to continue working in the same functional area after having been laid off by his former employer. He considered his work too dirty. More curious than serious, he interviewed at PC for a job. He liked what he saw when he walked through the plant, and he took the job. At that time, eight years prior to the study, four other people were working in the same area of production. He has worked alone for several years, performing a multitude of different functions of which he is proud and that he enjoys. It is his domain and he is essentially his own boss. He is running the department, which consists of him.

Three other people who had been self-employed prior to joining BIND mentioned that they were doubtful whether they could even work for somebody else. All three were surprised at how well they could, and perhaps they still feel as if they worked for themselves. One of them explains:

I was in business for myself for three years. I thought I was gonna have very big problems coming to work for a company, working *for* somebody, answering *to* someone, being here for a certain time to a certain time, being in a structured environment. And people tell me "how do you like working for someone now?" Well, I feel I'm working for myself.

The various observational data validated these verbal accounts about autonomy at work, which is supplemented by a strong work ethic. Observations revealed that organizational members across all levels and divisions are constantly productive. I almost felt out of place while waiting for a scheduled interview and sitting inactively among these busy people.

Organizational members do not abuse the provided autonomy. Instead they appreciate it as an opportunity to contribute and excel. One employee explains:

> People are more work oriented [as compared with another company where he had previously worked]. . . . I think there is a lot of enthusiasm in this company here to perform a lot.

Another employee provides this description:

> Management allows you to run with the ball. They don't put a lot of strict controls on you. They give you responsibility. . . . Although I report to a certain person and I do certain things, nobody really says "we want you to do this from now on differently, tomorrow you do this, the next day you do this . . ." I do make my own schedule. I do whatever I feel is necessary to get the job done. It's not like I have to say, so and so do this at 3 o'clock and at 4 o'clock you are supposed to do this . . . I make my own plan. They put confidence in me. And so far I've been successful. I've got good results for them and there is no reason to change that.
>
> I'm not monitored at all. I come in and I have the responsibility. I want to be here all day. I *want* to be here first thing in the morning. I want to be in the office. I don't want to take time off. I want to, and the reason is, I've been given, and it's up to me to succeed. . . . Maybe some people take advantage of that, but I don't want to do that. They have given me the opportunity to run my own show here.

Employees complement their autonomous efforts with various behaviors that integrate their individual activities. These can be characterized as team effort.

Team Effort

"I'm only as good as the people behind me." *Team effort* refers to activities that are intended to coordinate individual efforts and to integrate them so that a larger task is being accomplished. No formally structured events exist to achieve such an integration. Meetings occur between the people involved whenever a need emerges. Exchange of information happens constantly in an informal manner regardless of the position of people involved. Open doors are not a policy but a matter of course, which helps people get to each other quickly. Open doors help people know immediately whether somebody is in his or her office or whether he or she is in a meeting with somebody else. Doors are only shut if one needs quietness for a certain task or to ensure confidentiality in a conversation.

Frequent, informal encounters for information exchange help people to stay informed. They know what others around them are trying to accomplish. They know who is knowledgeable in which area and who to contact and ask for certain kinds of information. A telephone system has been designed and installed to encourage frequent calls with no additional costs between divisions located in different areas and regions and between divisions and the corporate office.

Both processes, autonomy and team effort, are accomplished in an efficient way. People exchange information in the most direct manner. If one person wants to know something, he or she goes directly to the person who has the needed information, or calls that person on the phone if he or she is located in a different division, rather than asking somebody else to get the information or having that person come to the office.

I could observe this behavior across all ranks. Workers on the shop floor would go to a coworker if they encountered a problem and they thought the other person could help. If inspectors find a problem in a certain dimension that can be corrected by a machine operator, they go to that person and explain the problem. In doing so the problem is solved immediately, where it occurs, rather than getting the plant manager or plant supervisor involved and having him pass on this information.

If shop-floor workers have a problem they feel is not attended to by the general manager, they may even call somebody at the corporate office, even the president. The president then gets back to the division and makes sure that the problem is being solved. The researcher was told at the PC division that this had happened, in the past, five or six times a year and that the employees then got what they had requested. This attention may, to some extent, be due to the fact that three of the current corporate officers come from this division. They still consider it to be the president's old company, and its former general manager had recently become a vice president.

At the managerial level team effort can be characterized not only as "MBWA" or "management by wandering around" but also as "MBGI" or "management by getting involved." The general manager at PC walks through the shop floor to find out himself who is working on which order and parts and what kind of progress is being made rather than having somebody bring him this information. The general manager at the GA division answers the phone and writes an order if customers call early in the morning when employees have not yet started working. The creation of the operations group is another example. The vice presidents visit their divisions on a regular basis, walk around, and participate in meetings. The president tries to "make his round" in each division once a year. "Getting involved in everything" is the respective guideline for behavior without, however, interfering with the responsibilities of others.

These examples illustrate the *informal way* of integrating and coordinating individual efforts and combining them in a joint project. This specific manner of accomplishing tasks is based on the special way in which people relate to each other. This constitutes another theme underlying directory knowledge.

PROCESS 2: RELATIONSHIPS AMONG PEOPLE

"We are very close, it's like a family." The theme *relationships among people* refers to the way people relate to each other and treat each other within the company. It includes both work and social interactions—personal encounters that are necessary to accomplish a task as well as voluntary or desired interactions with people. Relationships between people were deciphered by analyzing verbal and nonverbal components. Both are important indicators of the nature of relationships between people.

In general relationships among people at BIND can be characterized as informal, direct, open, and respectful with congruence in verbal and nonverbal behaviors. People behave authentically and deal with each other in an honest way. They generally mean what they say and follow-up on it with specific actions.[1]

Informality is expressed in verbal and nonverbal behavior, in the way people talk and behave with each other. They place strong emphasis on knowing each other's names across hierarchic levels. Respondents were irritated if they could not recall a person's name at once. Organizational members know each other, and each other's names, within the divisions. They address each other with first names even at the corporate office. Officers seem to know the names of at least the key people in the divisions they supervise. If they have or want to talk to a person and they run into him or her in the hallway, they exchange the information right there without scheduling a meeting or going into a special room unless it takes some time to discuss the issue. One person who had worked at the corporate office for 18 months described this informality as follows:

> In this company it's very casual. I came in and interviewed in a three-piece suit. In business, I figured. . . . And the president was in a Lacoste shirt! I said "Wait a minute! Wow!" I didn't know what to make of it. I felt uncomfortable. . . .
>
> This is the kind of company, and you don't have to—I'm not saying that you come in as a slob—but you can come in, you don't have to impress anyone. If you do a good job, if you work hard. It's not a dress-code per se. You don't have to wear a suit "cause you are in business." A lot of companies you would. . . .

Here you can be your own person. There are open communications. Everyone is treated equally. I call [the president] by his first name. Maybe some people refer to him by Mr. So and so, but I don't think it's disrespectful. I feel very close to them. I can go to X [a vice president, his supervisor] and I don't have to make an appointment . . .

And I think this informal attitude is healthy. It encourages me and it puts me on the same level that I can feel free to give my input. It creates creativity. People aren't afraid to think "I think that would be really a great idea but I can't tell him that." It's like management is here and you can say anything I feel like. If I have something to say to anybody I can walk in that door and say "I think that is a problem." I can discuss it person to person as my input and I think that's very important.

In addition to informality these accounts also express *directness* and *openness*, which could be observed in the way people talked and joked with each other on a personal level. Observations in all three divisions revealed that employees seem to know each other's personal side well. Their jokes and humor were predominantly personally oriented. People in the PC division talked back in the same manner they were addressed—even if status differences existed. One Friday afternoon, for example, one employee brought ice cream to the office. The general manager came in and saw the "office girls" eating. He told the heavier one that all she worried about was eating, and she replied something along the same lines. "We love our general. He doesn't love us all the time. Sometimes he does."

After he had gone she explained that they all were very close, like a family. And if somebody would talk to her like that, she had the right to talk back in the same way, even if it was the general manager. On the other hand her coworkers would be the first to help her—within reasonable limits—if she had a problem, if her car had broken down, or if she needed money.

To me it's the best [company], because you just like get along with everybody here, or everybody here is just so at ease, you know, you could talk to a person regularly, and if you feel like telling them what's on your mind, you tell them. Because they feel the same way, because it's not like nobody cuts everything in half. You say what you feel like, and it's vice versa. And they do it to you. That's why everybody is like, you get along better with somebody, and I'm telling you, . . . they take it and they not take it to be insulted by it, and they know. That's why we are so close, like, it's like a little family here, and basically that's what it is.

Another person explained that

you can't avoid getting involved when you work so closely with people day in day out, I mean getting involved in *everything*, not just your area, even when girlfriends call a married man.

Or at the GA division:

And we tease [the general manager]. We are the first to tell him when he makes a mistake 'cause he's the first to tell us when we make a mistake. But he takes it. But we also, we got to remember he's just like us. He's human, and you know he takes it. He's funny to work with. You crack up when you catch him making a mistake. And he tells me he's testing me, you know, "I was just testing you," "sure you were." . . . But if I need something done and I can't do it, I look for something that he may have, I go to him and ask him "did you see it." So I include him in my job and he includes me in his.

Employees not only practice this informality, openness, directness, and reciprocity in their relationships with their colleagues, boss, and subordinates, this kind of behavior is also typical for their relationships with customers, as the following account shows:

Be professional, I think that's really our criteria here. [Professional is considered to be] honesty, trust, verbal agreement. Human being agreement that used to be [in] the old terms old-gentleman's agreement between the client and the organization itself. Verbal contracting. Going back to the old ways rather than negotiating some types of forms. . . . It's always been personal relationship. Any entrepreneur, anybody who progresses onward has to have a personal relationship. You loose that humanistic value and you are just like everybody else. You are a figure, a social security number.

Respect is expressed toward people as human beings in their work roles. People who are knowledgeable and skilled in their areas are considered experts. When people's opinions are consulted, they carry weight. Once people are hired and kept beyond the 30-day trial period, they are entrusted with responsibilities and confidence and a certain freedom to do whatever they feel is necessary to best achieve the desired results. "As long as you are doing well and you are getting good results, there is no interference, you are allowed to go."

People respect the boundaries of their own territory, turf, or functional domain—whatever one may call it—and those of their coworkers. They go to the manager of another department first, if they have encountered a problem in his domain that requires detailed attention and that may involve decisions by him. They also know the boundaries of their own expertise. The interviewer was told several times to obtain certain information from another person who was considered better qualified in that area. Interviewees would even walk the interviewer to that person to get an answer or ask for an interview.

People tease and joke with each other but they don't "step" on each other personally so that somebody may be hurt. The acceptable boundaries regarding respect differ, however, for the divisions. People at PC treat each other in a rougher and tougher way than do people at the GA division or at the corporate headquarters. This difference is most likely due to the different nature of their work. The work at PC—especially on the shop floor—is physically hard, difficult, and rough.

The next theme refers to the way change and adaptation are accomplished so that the company stays viable.

PROCESS 3: ADAPTATION AND CHANGE

"There is always room for improvement." This theme refers to the company's way of responding to changes perceived in both their internal and their external environments. In general BIND's mode of change is characterized by combining and integrating two paradoxes: conservatism and innovative behavior. A change is only made if its outcome is proven and promises to be better in terms of reducing costs, time, and/or people's efforts. Guidelines for behavior are "no changes for the sake of change" or "if things are running smoothly we are not gonna upset the apple" cart. These two guidelines for behavior were mentioned in some way or another by most respondents.

Innovative behavior is shown in change behaviors that involve little or no substantial financial commitment and that help make work more efficient. *Conservatism* is demonstrated toward changes that involve substantial financial investments. They take into consideration only those capital-intensive changes that already have some proof of success inside or outside of BIND.

Internally the predominant mode of change across divisions is of an evolutionary rather than a revolutionary nature.[2] People adapt, change, and improve on an ongoing basis. When asked how they would make things better, one of the most frequent immediate responses was "there is always room for improvement." The analysis of recipe knowledge—strategies for improvement or repair strategies—demonstrated that organizational members behaved in these terms. Normative statements in the nature of "what we should do is . . ." were rare because BIND's people did and do whatever they need to do whenever they recognize that there is something they should do to obtain a certain outcome.

This ubiquitous nature of constant adaptations or changes made it initially difficult for respondents to think of major changes or innovations in the company. However, their verbal accounts were full of little changes taking place on an ongoing basis. Their way of thinking and behaving demonstrated continuous improvement of work processes to make work more efficient and to save money.

Changes that involve monetary investments are not as readily made. People need to sell them first to their general manager and then they need approval of the vice president in charge of the division. Such larger-scale changes are usually initiated through outside pressures. They are carefully investigated and weighed by several people. Decisions to proceed are not made quickly. A decision only finally happens if enough data suggest that a substantial amount of money will be saved or if it is a necessary investment for successful future competition.

Purchase of a new machine in the PC division is an example of such a change involving a large monetary investment. They bought their first numerical control machine after they had secured a substantial order for a job that could only be handled with such a machine. This existing order paid off a large amount of the investment. The machine turned out to be so successful in terms of precision and time, and eventually money saved that three other machines of the same type were bought during the next five years. A quality problem prompted the purchase of a coordinate measurement machine. This problem could not be detected with the conventional inspection tests conducted at PC. Despite this problem it took over a year of investigation and assurances before the decision was finally made to go ahead and buy the machine.

BIND only introduces something new, that has no well-established record of success, through successive experimentation, adaptation, and finally diffusion. They acquire experience in a first stage of testing that is confined to a "test center." They expect that limiting the experimentation with something new to one division will introduce the smallest amount of instability and the least amount of disturbance. Then if the experiment does not work out as expected, it has no negative effects beyond the boundaries of the test site. Once the results of experimentation are satisfactory, the new procedures or equipment are diffused to other divisions. Again diffusion occurs successively from one division to the next to keep the overall company as stable as possible.

Initiated by growing internal demands and external requirements from suppliers, the BIND business computer system was in the process of being changed in terms of both hardware and software. Once the decision was made about the hardware, software was developed in house. First they tested it in one of the company's divisions for a period of time. During the trial period they adjusted and optimized it on the basis of various suggestions from its users. Only then was it introduced in other divisions.

PROCESS 4: ACQUISITION AND PERPETUATION OF KNOWLEDGE

The theme *acquisition and perpetuation of knowledge* refers to processes of learning. More specifically it addresses two questions: How is new knowledge acquired and how is existing knowledge passed on to employees who do not have it yet? The first is necessary to stay competitive and keep up with external changes; the second refers to internal processes of preservation and institutionalization. Both processes are characterized at BIND by informality. While no differences exist across divisions in regard to the acquisition of knowledge, some differences emerge between the GA and the PC divisions in the way they perpetuate existing knowledge. These variations can be attributed to perceived differences in the nature of their work and in external conditions of the divisions.

Acquisition of New Knowledge

"Stay informed and stick out your neck." People from all three divisions try to stay informed about state-of-the-art trade knowledge by reading trade publications and by attending trade shows on a regular basis. They try to be aware of what their competitors are doing and listen to information from suppliers and customers that is brought back into the division by their sales people.

People at BIND usually hire employees beyond the shop-floor level with experience from the industry so that they do not require extensive training. People in technically skilled and managerial positions are expected to bring with them knowledge that is new to the division. This may also include some desired state-of-the-art knowledge to help improve work procedures at BIND and in the particular division. If a new need emerges and no insider has the needed knowledge, a search is conducted to find somebody with the respective qualifications and experience. "Get the best people" is one guideline for behavior expressed, enacted, and observed in all three divisions.

Perpetuation of Existing Knowledge

"Take your people along, educate and lead them." No formal training programs exist at either one of the studied divisions. Generally, existing knowledge is passed on in two ways: through informal coaching at work and through mentorship. New employees learn the ways things are and function at BIND by doing things in the same ways. They are shown some basics, they can observe, and they may ask their coworkers, but otherwise they are left on their own to explore, learn, understand, and make a contribution. The guideline "get the best people" is complemented by "let them swim." If they do something that does not bring about the desired results, they receive feedback. Expectations are clarified. These expectations refer to end results rather than the process of performing a certain function in a specific way. Most important is to do the right thing rather than doing that thing right. If the results are not satisfying the next time, their superior usually makes recommendations about how the desired results may be achieved. As mentioned before, employees are encouraged to think of new ways of doing things more cheaply without sacrificing quality. Depending on the scope of their functions, this attitude gives them freedom to experiment with different behaviors. As long as the desired results are achieved within the framework of acceptable behaviors or standards within BIND, there is no interference with *the way* these results are achieved.

Mentorship is a common way to pass on existing knowledge. Conditions are created so that people can develop both personally and professionally. Mentorship is predominantly practiced by officers and senior management. Knowing their key people, officers and senior managers are aware of current tasks, skills, strengths, needs, and shortcomings. In unobtrusive ways they entice their people to engage in projects that are of interest to them and that provide background for new experiences—for work-related learning as well as for personal growth. One executive officer describes it this way:

> I'm involved in many, many organizations outside of this. . . . It's a freebie sort of thing but I love to do it. And we are trying to teach the younger [employees] the same thing. I may use that term. . . . It's like with a child, you know, you try to help them out. . . . So I knew he was negatively involved [in a community project]. So when I saw this [another project] and I knew he was interested in it, I figured out he could get started from a level up here.

He continues talking about another person, specifying the same approach:

> I can see him being very good after a while. He needs a lot of hand-holding, which I'm doing now and I have X [another officer] do the same thing. We try to educate from down here [the corporate office]. . . . We don't take them by the hand, but we'll lead them, and we don't make any false promises. . . .
> We interviewed a couple of really sharp young gentlemen here today . . . and one was pushing me "where can I go from here?" I said "it's up to you." But what I'm saying is you get a good education. This is the main thing.

The above described processes underlying directory knowledge at BIND are embedded in a conducive and reinforcing environment. The data suggest that two parameters are prominent in creating this nurturing environment: the design of the company and the type of people working at BIND. Both constitute framing parameters or preconditions for the four processes to occur. In addition they provide the necessary control to make effective BIND's way of accomplishing tasks, their specific way of relating to each other, and their continuous adaptation. These two preconditions are described in the following section.

PRECONDITION I:
THE NATURE OF ORGANIZATIONAL MEMBERS

"We need initiators, we need people who are willing to take responsibility and who are willing to work hard." The people who work at BIND have certain characteristics in common. Job applicants are deliberately screened for these characteristics, and individuals who do not have them seem either to be terminated or to resign after the 30-day trial period. This screening procedure represents a subtle but strong process of control that starts at the company level and cascades through the entire organization. Only those companies with a successful financial track record and a certain type of management style are acquired. BIND acquires a new firm *because* of its management and its employees. Management has to be willing to stay with the company for at least five years after the acquisition is completed. Owners who sell their companies to BIND have to be genuinely concerned about their employees and treat them with respect; this is described by the president:

> You don't have to fight with people in order to get them to do a good job. I think that's more detrimental. We insist that they review their people regularly, talk with them, try.

This respect toward employees, including their fair treatment, is delineated in policies regarding the treatment of personnel. These policies are enacted and role modeled by top management and corporate services. Executive officers are easily accessible to all employees regardless of their positions. Telephone calls are not screened. The internal audit group is also instructed to gather data about this nonrecorded human side of management in the divisions.

If there is an indication of a violation, the president will intervene, no matter how minor it is. For example, the internal audit manager had once found that a married employee had filed for tax withholding in single status. The division's controller explained that it was that employee's explicit wish. The audit manager kept the issue in the report for the executive officers. The president called the controller after reading it. He was upset about this "error" that kept some money from the employee. The employee then had to explain the issue directly to the president.

During his visits at each division, the president tries to find out himself about the personal atmosphere by talking to people and sensing whether they are afraid to talk to him:

> I think I have a good sense of the kind of people and I know when I go into a place. I can sense it if people are afraid to talk to me or guarding to look around. You know, there are a lot of little indicators. Then if I sense that I pursue it a little bit further. Although we have the vice presidents who keep in close touch with the companies [divisions]. It's not just me.

At the corporate office the president has arranged health education and stress reduction programs for the employees. One office is permanently designated to a community group working for disarmament, and BIND has adopted a high school. Different people from BIND assist students in their projects. A vice president may give a lecture about various aspects of business, or an employee experienced in personnel matters may spend a day with graduating students to help them write résumés and train them in interviewing skills.

In addition to this human side, a certain approach toward work is desired in people. This approach was validated by both interview and observational data. People working at BIND take initiative, take action, experiment, take responsibility, work hard, and are ambitious. Potential hires are carefully screened for these characteristics. Formal education is not important. What counts are actions, ideals, and initiative. One of the vice presidents explains:

> Not necessarily the fact that someone goes to college they are gonna be better or worse than somebody else, which I found is never always so. Our so-called . . . guy has never gone to college and I wouldn't trade him for 25 college graduates.

Positions throughout the company are filled with entrepreneurially oriented people exemplified by the president. He expressed that all his life he preferred "doing things his way" rather than working for somebody else and having to conform to somebody else's standards and expectations. After having finished his engineering degree while working part-time to earn some money and to get experience in the field, he went into business with a friend. Several of the other interviewees did not finish school or a degree program they had started. They instead left school to get experience or had started their own businesses.

The combination of a humanistic orientation with an attitude of "doing it his way" seems to have made BIND's president sensitive to the needs of people who think like he does. Top management grants general managers the necessary freedom to act in their way if they show concern about people and are not afraid of work. Several general managers who did not and could not work under these conditions left or had to leave. The president recalls:

A few months ago I let a man go because he was overbearing, autocratic and created a sense of fear, making people afraid of him. I'm not comfortable with that.

General managers are described as decision makers. One of the executive officers told a story about a general manager who had decided—against the vice president's advice—to make an investment that did not result in the expected return within three years. The officer in charge brought it to his attention. No blaming or direct punishment occurred except a reduction in bonus based on the lower return on investment. The officer feels that he would rather have people make a wrong decision than no decision. General managers are action takers,

short sleeve dig-in type of people. That's been the background of the managers in this division. They are also frank in voicing their opinion. . . . They are doers. They go out and get involved in things, they *do* things. . . . BIND has been very successful in the people that they do hire. . . . They have been lucky to capture good managers.

The major recruiter at BIND described the type of people he was looking for as aggressive, bright, intelligent, ambitious, sincere:

The *All* American. We do hire a lot of foreigners, too, but you look for the person who really is on the ball plus people who have experience are on the ball. Not the people who give you a weak handshake, kind of soft-spoken. Those are not getting anywhere in the company.

People who are hired are outspoken and make suggestions. Making an improvement almost has the quality of an initiation rite. It is considered such a ubiquitous part of daily work activities that the newly hired seem compelled to take such an action to achieve a sense of belonging. Making an improvement seems to provide the feeling that they are an accepted member of the division. All the respondents that were recently hired pointed out such an improvement. In addition they expressed pride and admiration that they could make an impact.

The analysis of recipe knowledge—normative-causal knowledge about improvements and repair strategies—revealed that this initiating and action-taking attitude is a part of everyday work activities for longer-term employees. There were only few accounts in the nature of "what we really should do to make things better here is xyz." In general people felt that, whenever they saw a need for something to change, improve, or get done, they would do it right then and there. Or they referred to changes that were in the process of being designed and/or implemented. Instead of "should's," they mostly expressed desires that were beyond their functional domains. These tended to involve decisions at a higher level such as investments in the physical work environment, a larger facility, or, in one case, more attention to certain managerial functions.

The control process of selecting this "special" kind of person is, to a large extent, a subtle self-selection process. It can be characterized by "hiring in their own image." Executive officers make sure that a general manager has those characteristics about which they feel strongly. General managers then tend to hire and promote people who—in addition to having technical knowledge or expertise—exhibit similar characteristics. This notion was supported by the main recruiter's reported practices as well as by observations at all three research sites. A former general manager of PA, who is now a vice president, selected several key people who are similar to him and who show similar characteristics among each other. They are all aggressive, action takers, fighters, ambitious and they want to accomplish things fast. The manager of electronic subsystems was quite different: more quiet, reserved, and almost shy. He did not seem to be pressed for time even when he talked about his large work load. This division had not been developed at PC. Instead it had been moved from another division to the PC division. This "different" manager had just hired another person who showed similar characteristics that could also be found among the workers in his division. This contrast in managers and people are also mirrored by the different nature of their work. While the work on PC's shop floor requires a fast pace, the work in electronic subsystems needs patience as well as precise and calm movements.

Another precondition or organizational control mechanism that allows and nurtures this hands-on, personal style of management, which lets employees be initiators, is the design of the company.

PRECONDITION II: ORGANIZATIONAL DESIGN

"Centralize as little as possible." "If you want people to pay attention to something, don't take the responsibility away from them." Organizational design refers to the structure of BIND, its formal components of delineating responsibilities, coordination, and control. Several dimensions can be found in the literature to describe structure such as division of labor, hierarchy, extent of bureaucratization, centralization, formalization, and differentiation.[3] The design at BIND can be characterized by flat, small within large, loose coupling within a few tight parameters and adhocracy. It shows a minimum of centralization, formalization, and virtually no bureaucratization.

At the time of the study, BIND consisted of 2,500 employees located in 30 divisions including the corporate office. Divisions had a "standard size" of 80 to 100 people. This standard size was consciously chosen. Top management felt that their desired management style—characterized by a people orientation and strong personal involvement with maximum control through direct leadership—is only possible in a small-sized company. The general manager should be able to walk through his facility within one to two minutes and know what is happening. Furthermore they felt that small divisions within an overall large company create more opportunities for people through increased possibilities for vertical promotion. With such a design more positions are available into which people can move up.

Two exceptions to the standard size existed at the time of the study, and the exceptions supported management's basic theory. These were the corporate office, which employed 25 people, and one manufacturing division in Northern California. The Northern California manufacturing division had grown within a few years from BIND's standard size. Its splitting up was debated at the time of the study. Such a splitting or the development of subsidiaries represents a common growth pattern among BIND's distribution divisions. Once a subsidiary is large enough to function independently, it is decoupled. Nine months after completion of the study, I visited the corporate headquarters to collect some additional data and learned that, instead of splitting the Northern California division, they had decided to size it down to BIND's standard size. Various problems had occurred in that division due to its size that had made top management realize—and accept—the limits of their desired management style.

The overarching design parameter of BIND's structure is to centralize only as much as necessary and to decentralize as much as possible. Centralization is achieved through the corporate office, which defines itself as a service division for BIND's divisions. Standards, policies, and services that have been developed at the corporate office include matters of finance; aspects of human resource management, such as health care plans, benefits, profit sharing plans, and general rules of conduct toward employees; accounting procedures; and facility maintenance or real estate transactions. Legal services, assistance with the BIND business computer system, and recruiting services have been added to the services that can, but do not have to, be used by the divisions.

Financial matters are tightly controlled on a weekly and monthly basis. Each division has to give its cash status and its projected needs for the next week on Friday so that the surplus can be invested by the corporate office. This reporting system ensures that top management has information about major investments made by divisions.

Expenses, accounting procedures, and aspects of human resource management are specified in the policy manual. They delineate BIND's "no frills management," such as traveling by coach and using public transportation whenever available and appropriate for the business situation. The policy manual gives some general guidelines for conducting a fair job interview— what is considered appropriate to ask and what is not. New employees receive an employee handbook that informs them about their rights and duties and the expectations BIND has for them.

Enactment of policies and procedures is controlled and reinforced by the internal audit group. Its members review each division every other year. They discuss their observations with the general manager and controller before they hand their report over to the officers for review. People at the corporate office consider their office to be a role model for the divisions. They try to keep their staff and their expenses at a minimum. Executive officers do not have private secretaries. They do not take for themselves privileges that they would not grant, for example, to a general manager.

In addition to these policies and procedures that are controlled tightly, divisions have freedom in *how* they achieve the expected results. Goals are set jointly with a vice president. But, as long as their performance is satisfactory, there is no intervention by the corporate office. "As long as things are running smoothly we are not gonna upset the apple cart", as one of the corporate officers expressed it. Each division can find its own formula to achieve success and enact it without being bothered by the corporate office in terms of *how* to run its business. One of the general managers expressed this as follows:

> I have a free hand as long as the bottom line is good—return on investment, and profit, and growth. They pretty much leave us alone. They are there any time we have a question, they are there for answers and for help. They [in the corporate office] are super about that. I mean, it isn't like "we just leave you guys alone." That isn't the case at all. But it's an excellent situation. We have full freedom pretty much to do what we want—as long as it turns out right.

Only when performance indicators slip below expectations over a period of time are recommendations jointly developed by the corporate officers for that division. If the overall performance of the division still does not improve, an officer or another person sent by the corporate office may assist the general manager on a daily basis. The corporate deputy is both to help the general manager and to find out in more detail what kind of problems exist and where they are located. If a division continues to be unprofitable over a period of three years and if several efforts indicate that the division cannot be turned around, it is sold.

Nevertheless these direct interventions are considered exceptions to the guidelines rather than standard. This "intervention by exception" guideline is enabled by the type of people working at BIND; it involves control through careful selection procedures rather than more direct control through bureaucratic rules and regulations.

SUMMARY

An analysis of directory knowledge—process knowledge regarding how things get done—has revealed cultural synergism. The cultural groupings that form according to perceived functional domains in regard to dictionary knowledge did not translate into directory knowledge. Four common processes were found to underlie organizational members' actions across different departments and different divisions in accomplishing innovation or change in the company. These commonly found processes refer to the way tasks are accomplished, to relationships among people, to adaptation and change, and to the acquisition and perpetuation of knowledge. People at BIND accomplish their tasks through a combination of individual autonomy and team effort enacted in an efficient way. Relationships among people—both insiders and outsiders, such as customers—can be characterized in terms of informality, directness, openness, and respect. BIND achieves both adaptation and change through innovative behavior and conservatism. Improvements are made on an ongoing basis, especially if they do not require substantial financial commitments. If such commitment is required, people show conservatism in adopting new technologies or processes that have already proven successful. Changes are made, introduced, and adjusted through controlled and successive experimentation.

People acquire new knowledge predominantly in two ways: by hiring new people who have the desired knowledge and by staying informed about technical changes in the industry. People stay informed by reading trade publications and by regularly attending trade shows. They perpetuate already existing knowledge through informal coaching on the job and through mentorship. Top management in particular, in subtle ways, provides opportunities for managers to develop and grow.

I found that two parameters create this environment: one is the nature of organizational members and the other is the company's design. New employees are carefully selected—consciously and subconsciously—to fit the desired and existing nature of employees: to take initiative, to be willing to take responsibility, and to work hard.

The company's design—small within large with much autonomy at the divisional level—creates "intrapreneurship." It helps entrepreneurs stay within BIND and accomplish tasks and changes as described.

In the next chapter I report findings about recipe knowledge. In this particular company recipe knowledge was closely related to directory knowledge.

NOTES

1. Authentic behavior has been characterized by Rogers (1961).
2. Greiner (1979) explains these two modes of change in detail.
3. Scott (1981) describes, for example, various forms of organizational design.

SEVEN

Findings About Recipe Knowledge

Recipe knowledge is defined as cultural knowledge about recommendations, improvements, and repair strategies. It is composed of cognitions about what should be done to improve things or what should be done in case something goes awry.

The data which I obtained about recipe knowledge were somewhat limited as compared to the data obtained in regard to the other kinds of cultural knowledge. A critical examination of potential reasons revealed that this was mostly due to the nature of the selected firm, that is, a sampling bias at the organizational level. Nevertheless, several new insights resulted from the data analysis of this kind of cultural knowledge. These results are, however, the most tentative ones and need further investigation. First of all, two different aspects of recipe knowledge emerged. One refers to recommendations with an "ought to" or "should" nature as defined above. The other one delineates recommendations and improvement strategies which have proven successful or unsuccessful and which are therefore recommended to continue to do or to avoid. In regard to themes and cultural groupings, the results of the data analyses were in some respects associated with the results obtained in the analysis of dictionary knowledge and in others with the results obtained in regard to directory knowledge.

At the recipe level of knowledge, four different themes emerged which I labeled *acting vs. talking about acting, time frame, approach to change,* and *problem areas.* One reoccurring theme emerged across hierarchical levels, divisions, and functional domains. It dealt with *acting* in terms of improving rather than talking about what should be improved. This theme was of the nature "continue to do." Two interrelated themes emerged in regard to the *time frame* and to their *approach to change.* The former one implied to do things faster while the latter recommended predominantly less cautious behavior toward change. Both themes had a "should" nature and reflected changes away from the present state. In regard to these two themes, cultural groupings seemed to form according to perceived functional domains as well as personal concerns. Furthermore, the content of recipe knowledge tended to be influenced by hierarchical levels, the nature of employees, and the nature of work.

One other theme emerged only in one of the divisions and dealt with several problem areas that were present at the time of the study. This theme had the nature of "should" and was influenced by the specific situation in that division.

Factors which tended to maintain cultural groupings in regard to recipe knowledge were the degree of autonomy which organizational members have, the pre-selection of organizational members and organizational design.

THE NATURE OF RECIPE KNOWLEDGE

A critical analysis of the data obtained in regard to recipe knowledge suggests that the above given definition of recipe knowledge needs further specification. More precisely, the recipe knowledge which surfaced in this study fell into two different categories: some of it had the nature of lessons which interviewees learned from past behavior. They implied a continuing use of certain behaviors or avoiding the use of certain behaviors. These lessons could be either lessons about successful outcomes or lessons about unsuccessful outcome. I refer to the former ones as recipes of success and the latter ones as recipes of failure. An example of a recipe of success in BIND is "improve whenever you see a need for it." A recipe of failure is "don't acquire troubles companies."

The results obtained from recipe knowledge with the "do" or "avoid to do" nature are closely related to the findings about directory knowledge in terms of cultural groupings and the variables which tend to influence the content of cultural groupings and their knowledge as well as the factors maintaining cultural groupings. At least the major recipe of success ("improve whenever you see a need for it") was present in all three divisions cutting across different functional domains, hierarchical levels, and divisional boundaries. Other recipes of success or failure were mostly mentioned by only one or two people. Thus, they represent personal experiences or concerns and their content tends to be influenced by the nature of their work. The major difference between such a recipe of success and directory knowledge is the prescriptive rather than descriptive quality of a recipe.

The results about the recipe knowledge with the nature of "should" as originally defined is closer related to the findings in regard to dictionary knowledge. This aspect of recipe knowledge implies recommendations about changing the current state of being. It suggests that different kinds of behavior may be in order for a higher level effectiveness or smooth running. I refer to this nature of recipe knowledge as recipe *for* success. Three themes with the nature of "should" emerged in different locations. Due to their nature, I labeled them *time frame, approach to change,* and *problem areas*. The theme *time frame* recommends that things should be done faster, especially the introduction of changes. The theme *approach to change* suggests that BIND should be less cautious and more willing to take risks, whereas the theme *problem areas* suggests certain changes of conditions which are perceived less than optimal.

Similar to dictionary knowledge, cultural groupings which emerged in regard to recipe knowledge with the nature of "should" tended to form according to perceived functional domains (time frame, approach to change, problem areas). In addition, some cultural groupings formed according to division (e.g., problem areas). The major difference between recipe knowledge with the nature of "should" and dictionary knowledge is also its prescriptive rather than descriptive quality.

The following sections discuss each of the themes in turn including the respective cultural groupings. The reader should, however, keep in mind the tentative nature of these results.

DO-THEME: ACTING VERSUS TALKING ABOUT ACTING

This theme which was present in all three divisions was most likely responsible for the limited amount of data which surfaced in regard to recipe knowledge. In this particular company, people improve whenever they see a need for it. And they do it in a way which I already described in regard to dictionary knowledge. A common response was "If I would think of anything to make better, I would do it." This theme was so pervasive that several interviewees mentioned improvements which they had initiated and implemented. The difference in comparison to dictionary knowledge is, however, that this theme has a prescriptive rather than merely descriptive nature. "Improve whenever you see a need for it" is a lesson of success which is passed on to new members of the organization.

Similar to the findings in regard to directory knowledge, the cultural grouping in regard to the recipe of success "continue to do" seemed to cross divisional, hierarchical as well as functional domain boundaries. We can therefore hypothesize that this group exists company-wide within BIND.

The major single factor which contributed to this formation of a cultural synergism is, again, the selection procedure of employees within BIND. Chapter 6 described already this pre-selection process for certain behaviors in regard to directory knowledge. Without this pre-selection procedure, which acts as an organizational and cultural control mechanism, it is most likely that cultural groupings will form according to divisional boundaries and/or perceived functional domains.

SHOULD-THEME: TIME FRAME

The recipe theme *time frame* has a "should" nature. Interviewees who mentioned it implied that the same things should be done faster. They felt that most of the decisions that had been made and implemented during the past 12 years were good but they should have been done faster. One interviewee expressed it in terms of the actual decision making, another in terms of more pervasiveness, so that things would happen faster. Some of the interviewees recognized, however, that the amount of time involved in doing thins at BIND depends on the company's decentralized structure, that is, one of the preconditions discussed in Chapter 6. The existing operating and decision making processes within BIND provide opportunities. In regard to time, they are, however, a definite trade-off.

Seven of the ten interviewees from HQ mentioned this theme in one way or another whereas only two of the thirty interviewees from PC mentioned it and none of the interviewees from the GA division. It seems therefore that carriers of this recipe are predominantly located at the corporate office.

Several factors indicated that the content of this theme is influenced by a combination of hierarchy and power center in terms of decision making power. First, this theme was not only mentioned by the top management group but also by some of the corporate officers who mentioned this theme. And second, those people who mentioned the theme in the PC division had contact with the respective people at HQ. This hypothesis needs, however, further investigation.

SHOULD-THEME: APPROACH TO CHANGE

The recipe theme *approach to change* has also a "should" nature and is related to the theme *time frame*. The interviewees who mentioned it implied that BIND as a company and more precisely its top and middle management behave too cautiously that they are too reluctant to change. Respondents who mentioned this theme felt that management was too reluctant to change, that they should become more proactive and more risk taking. Or as several interviewees expressed it in regard to decisions about technological issues such as a computer system "go more with the times."

If we relate this recipe "we should be less cautious to change" to some of the results in regard to directory knowledge, this recipe does not come as a total surprise. In analogy to the above theme *time frame*, some of the BIND's directory knowledge prohibits its carriers from changing more quickly. As Chapter 6 describes, decision making processes and changes fall into two different categories—those which involve hardly any financial resources and those which require substantial financial resources. The former changes are introduced on an ongoing basis while the latter ones are only introduction *after* they have proven successful elsewhere.

A closer examination of the examples which interviewees gave in regard to this theme support these considerations. Most of the changes which had happened too slowly were connected with financial resources such as BIND's computer system, the modernization of their trucks, expansion and/or renovation of offices or production spaces, etc. Despite these specific examples, respondents generalized this theme and suggested in general that BIND should be less cautious in terms of its change behavior.

Interviewees from all three divisions mentioned this theme: four from HQ, one from PC, and five from GA. At closer inspection of the interview data, it appear that the theme is predominantly held by people who belong to the same functional domain groupings as differentiated in regard to dictionary knowledge. But again, these findings are rather tentative and need further investigation.

SHOULD-THEME: PROBLEM AREAS

The recipe theme *problem areas* has also the nature of "should." It refers to specific problems which some of the interviewees perceived at the time of the study predominantly in one of the three divisions (PC). More specifically, several respondents mentioned four different problem areas of which two are highly interrelated. One deals with communication problems, another with general management or rather the general manager of PC, the third with insufficient management information and management control systems, and the fourth with better physical work place conditions.

Communication problems resulted predominantly on the basis of perceived functional domain groupings. Members who belonged to different functional domain groupings within PC felt that communications and interactions should improve between the members of the different groups. At the time of the study, the members of each grouping took their breaks at different times, mingled in different areas, and stuck mostly with their own functional domain grouping. That is, the groups sustained their systems. This fostered in turn their own identity and separated them at the same time from the other groupings. This problem area was mentioned by eight of the interviewees from PC.

Given the fact that PC had a high percentage of Spanish speaking workers at the shop floor level (production grouping), one may wonder if language difficulties contributed to this communication problem. Some of the interview data revealed however, that this was no longer the case. In former years, members from the shop floor production grouping found it difficult to communicate with management due to language problems. This problem disappeared when a bilingual engineer became head of production. In addition, hierarchy seemed to be of a less contributing factor when compared to the qualities of the highest ranking person in PC.

Several interviewees identified general management as a problem area. They felt that the behavior of the general manager should change—both in regard to internal as well as external issues. According to six respondent, his way of managing the PC division was mainly an extension of his former behavior in his position as production control manager. Instead of managing, controlling behavior dominated his thinking and acting both at an interpersonal and at a factual level.

Respondents who mentioned this theme belonged predominantly to one functional domain grouping (lower management of PC) but it was also mentioned by members of the production grouping.

Related to this problem, some interviewees considered the (non-)existence of a management information/control system as a recipe for success (three). All three belonged to the same functional domain grouping and perceived this problem from the basis of their work.

Seven interviewees at PC mentioned physical aspects of the work place as a "should" recipe. The carriers of this recipe for success belonged to different production groupings, mostly the shop-floor grouping. Respondents felt that they should have more room, air conditioning, and a cleaner place. These concerns are to some extent related to the shop-floor grouping's spatial location in between the electronics and the inspection groupings. The nature of the work of both of these groupings require much cleaner work environments. This is especially true of the electronics grouping, whose equipment needs a stable room temperature. The constant confrontation with the "better" work environment of these two groupings has most likely led to this recipe for success.[1]

In the analysis of recipe knowledge, I wondered why so little recipe knowledge emerged in comparisons to the other kinds of cultural knowledge. In the course of the study, I explored several potential reasons for this, including the interviewing procedures and response biases. The most obvious one would be that the interviewing procedure was not sensitive enough to surface recipe knowledge. My probing questions in regard to recipe knowledge did, however, not trigger more information about general recommendations and suggestions for improvements or repair. Other reasons for the little amount of data could be systematic response biases. Interviewees could withhold information either voluntarily or involuntarily. A critical examination revealed that the latter was the case. Due to the nature of the company, its pre-selection of organizational members and thus the special nature of the people working in this firm, little recipe knowledge had accumulated.

Despite the tentative findings based on the limited amount of recipe knowledge, I still consider it an important aspect of cultural knowledge in organizations. In this company, the recipes of success and failure are closely related to directory knowledge, that is, knowledge about processes whereas the recipes *for* success are more closely related to dictionary knowledge. At the same time, internal political behavior seemed to be absent. Rather than trying to foster their individual interests at the potential expense of others, people helped each other out within the framework of their family feeling. One may hypothesize that recipe and directory knowledge differ from each other in companies in which internal politics operate to a larger extent. Under such conditions, the amount of recipe knowledge with a "should" nature is most likely larger. These questions need to be addressed in future research.

The last three chapters described, analyzed, and explained dictionary, directory, and recipe knowledge. These chapters referred to interpretations of what exists in the company, to everyday theories of action about how to make things happen, and what should be done to improve them. The interviews conducted have also revealed some information about axiomatic knowledge that gives insight into the *why* of things. The following chapter describes these axioms or assumptions and their implications.

NOTE

1. This comparison which may happen on a daily basis is most likely a demotivating factor as defined by Herzber, Mausner, and Snyderman (1959).

EIGHT

Axiomatic Knowledge: Culture Formation and Institutionalization

Some of the interviews revealed several basic assumptions that have influenced BIND's existence as a company. Because of their axiomatic nature, I have labeled the respective knowledge *axiomatic*. More specifically these axioms have influenced the creation and perpetuation of BIND—its identity, aspirations, strategies, structure, and various operations. These assumptions surfaced in interviews conducted with the president and vice presidents—that is, those people who created the company in its current form, the key decision makers who actively took part in the restructuring process which started 12 years prior to the study.

As mentioned above BIND had acquired about 18 companies within a four-year period in the mid-1960s. Its former president, a sales-oriented person, acquired one company after another for stock and attempted to create a centralized organization. His plan did not, however, work out. The stock of BIND plummeted. And the managers of the large divisions started to worry because all they had received in return for their companies was stock. The president of BIND finally resigned for personal reasons. The person who succeeded him was the general manager of the PC division, the largest individual shareholder.

Faced with the plummeting stock, the new president gathered those people who were in the same situation as he was. They sat down and had "some philosophical discussions," as the president expressed it. Several assumptions and guidelines were debated by this group of people. Together they wanted to "devise some approach to management that made sense" as the president recalls. The further development, restructuring, and turnaround of BIND were based on these negotiated and agreed upon assumptions and guidelines.

This group discussed and negotiated assumptions in regard to business operations, organizational design, managerial skills of the division's management, future economic development, and organizational members of BIND. The personal beliefs of the president, and his experience and practices in his own company, had a strong influence on the assumptions and guidelines that finally emerged from these discussions. The resulting set of axioms served as a foundation for the company's shape and future existence.

Subsequent successes validated the appropriateness of these basic axioms. Some of them were further adjusted, refined, or revised through critical evaluation of actions taken and growing experience. In addition management used the above described selection processes for organizational members as a control mechanism to ensure that their beliefs were maintained and disseminated throughout the company. People—especially in key positions—are carefully selected and screened for these cherished beliefs and practices. Once hired they are closely examined during the 30-day probation period.

While the top management group discussed and negotiated the assumptions and guidelines for BIND in the face of perceived problems, BIND's policies emerged as the result of recurring problems. They were formulated to emphasize and reinforce major concerns of the management group.

The following section outlines the assumptions that were discussed by top management. The reader will discover that these assumptions represent a limited and selective choice among several alternatives. Another top management group who found themselves in a similar situation but who held different beliefs might have made a different choice.

THE FORMATION PROCESS
WITH ITS ASSUMPTIONS

Controlling the Company and
Its Business Environment

First BIND's new management group needed to find a measure to indicate which divisions were worth retaining and which were not. Before the change in management the most important measure and guideline for behavior was percentage of sales. The new group felt that this was an inadequate measure for comparing a diverse group of companies. They finally agreed that return on equity was a better criterion to use to decide whether or not the performance of a division was sufficient. Growing experience helped them further specify this measure for comparing the results of their different divisions.

In their efforts to stabilize the company and to make its relevant business environment more predictable, they also had to decide in which business they wanted to be. They finally realized that style-oriented products such as carpets, furniture, or boats were more difficult to manage for them. They attributed these difficulties to changes in taste and style that made the business environment less predictable. They also assumed the external environment would continue to be cyclical. To achieve overall stability at BIND in such a cyclical environment, they felt that a well-balanced approach with a focus on only a few select product areas was most appropriate. As a result they retained only four product areas, which were either in production or in distribution.

Over the years of gaining experience, their focus of growth shifted increasingly to the distribution of products even though most of the corporate officers came from a production area. They expected highest profitability from this product area as well as the most potential for future growth. A further step toward stability represented their decision to sell to companies rather than to individual consumers. They had experienced that individual consumers—as compared with major companies—have less predictable buying patterns. In addition individual consumers are more easily influenced by recessions.

Making Money

Another related change concerned employees' attitudes regarding sales. They replaced the prior focus on sales quantities by a focus on quality sales and a profit orientation. "Make only good sales" or "profitable sales" became a guideline for behavior for sales people as well as for general managers. They accomplished this change by redesigning or creating compensation, reward, and incentive systems. These systems were all part of the changes they made in terms of the design of the company.

Organizational Design

The new management group needed to develop a new organizational design or structure for the company. This design had to be appropriate for the diverse group of divisions that they retained under the umbrella of BIND. They felt that the design should support rather than contradict the guidelines developed for conducting business at BIND. One of the executive officers recalls:

There was no organization. There really was no, no organization at the time we came in. There was no such a thing. Everybody was well, you know, "we are gonna buy this company" and buy the company. . . . We set up criteria which wasn't done before in that way, even though it was a public corporation. . . . We initiated the whole format, let's call it an organizational format. That's something that we had innovated, initiated here, or whatever, and we think it's pretty good. . . . Well, we have proven it out.

They finally developed a decentralized, loosely coupled structure for BIND. This design was based on the following assumption, which was influenced by the president's personal beliefs: If companies had been worthy enough to be acquired by BIND, they still must have enough managerial skills to manage their own business because all employees and management were retained. Based on this assumption several responsibilities that had been centralized at the corporate office were given back to each division's management. The president explains: "So we decided to turn back all the accounting to them and to put back everybody in business for themselves, with certain limitations."

Corporate Responsibility

The limitations concerned financial matters. The president felt that he and the vice presidents in their role as executive officers held dual responsibilities: one to the shareholders of BIND and the other to BIND's employees. Shareholders should not be disappointed in their trust in BIND, and the company should provide a secure workplace for its employees. They felt that they could be most successful in their dual responsibility by creating tight and central controls for financial matters in addition to social control processes. The corporate office would invest the profits of all divisions and reinvest according to each division's return on investments. The president explains:

So we killed two birds with one [stone]. . . . We gave them back their business to run and one condition was that all the excess cash came into the corporate office. And if they need anything, they would ask for it. We would consider the request and give it to them. . . .

So the corporate officers in essence manage cash. That was our job. We looked at ourselves as portfolio managers with a bunch of investments and to be realistic about it. The only difference was, we did have some management skills, and some technical experience in each of these areas. We were more than just the typical portfolio manager. We could give them advice, we could help them and guide them and direct them, but not take responsibility of management. . . .

And we made it quite clear that they had to be honest with us if they wanted to run their own business. And most of them were entrepreneurs and would have left at the completion of the contract [concerning the acquisition] if we did change the environment.

They established additional—social—controls through a careful selection process for key personnel. Top management preselects, for example, the controllers to be hired by a division, and they approve general managers and their successors. They also have created an internal audit group—formerly called "goodwill ambassadors"—to reinforce established policies at the division level.

People

The top management group discussed and made assumptions concerning the people working at BIND. They also established guidelines—influenced by the president's personal beliefs—that delineate how employees should be treated. They assumed that people work hard if they are appropriately rewarded for the results, that people pay attention to what they are held responsible for, that BIND's managers and employees are human beings with emotional needs, and that everybody is in business together. These four assumptions guided them in their design of reward and incentive structures, of fringe benefits, and of means for symbolic recognition as well as in the design of jobs.

People at BIND consider their pay to be good, at least in skilled and managerial positions. Bonuses and profit sharing plans reward their performance and encourage their identification with the company's major goal of controlled profitable growth. The incentive system at PC is designed so that workers can double or even triple their wages if they put in the effort. But they also need to pay attention to criteria that are considered important by management, such as efficiency without loss of quality. Work schedules are flexible in terms of additional hours that give workers the opportunity to further increase their income.

This implicit contract regulates the relationships between management and workers. It can be described as follows: "If you put in your effort we show our recognition." This implicit contract is also reflected in the profit sharing plan. Employees first have to show their willingness by contributing a certain percentage of their income. Management will then contribute the larger portion to demonstrate their recognition.

Management expresses their recognition further in several symbolic ways: through luncheons, Christmas parties, trips to Disneyland, trips to football or baseball games, an opportunity to go to a trade show in a different country, the yearly general managers' meeting in a nice resort area, or trophies presented by the president to general managers for the best performances in areas that are considered important by top management.

Jobs are designed in a flexible way. People can move and are moved around to find the jobs they like best and in which they can do best. All respondents with more than one year of tenure had already performed several different functions within one or even several divisions. Workers are cross-trained to avoid layoffs in recessionary times. A side effect of this cross-training is that workers express pride in their diverse skills and their autonomy to change workstations when they see a need. As a result BIND does not have a formal organization chart. People are encouraged to "do what they do best." Jobs are adjusted to people, to their strengths and shortcomings. Management searches for ways to compensate for shortcomings. If a general manager is, for example, strongly sales oriented, he will be counterbalanced by a strong controller. The president explains:

> I don't have an organization chart. I don't like to put things in big boxes. I try to, I like to have a little flexibility. But don't mistake that for that we are not being well organized. It's just, I don't like to draw a picture and let people think that that's where they fit. You understand. So I don't do that. In my mind, many times, I do, I'll make a chart for my own purposes, and look at it and then tear it up. . . .
>
> We usually avoid having an accountant as a manager. We try to avoid having a salesman as a manager because both of them—the accountant is too numbers oriented and the salesman is too sales oriented. So we try to strike something in between. We try to strike a balance. . . . If we had somebody who is weak in sales, a manager who doesn't have much personal interest in sales may be a good people manager, but he isn't particularly sales oriented, be sure that he has a very strong salesman. Now we don't do the hiring, you know, we'll discuss it, encourage . . . our opinion to be held.

Structural parameters reinforce existing processes of social control. Both ensure that the executive officers' opinion is followed. Management also use them to maintain and perpetuate cultural knowledge, which I will discuss in the following section.

INSTITUTIONALIZING CULTURAL KNOWLEDGE

Analysis of interview and observational data suggest that two social control mechanisms institutionalize cultural knowledge and maintain and perpetuate it: One is through recruiting people with the "right attitude" and the other one is through coaching and mentorship. Both processes are enforced and reinforced through design parameters. Among them are corresponding control and reward systems and symbolic recognition, which have been described above.

Recruiting people with the "right attitude," and their coaching and mentoring, seem to play the most prominent roles in the process of passing on cultural knowledge. People are deliberately selected who exhibit the same attitudes, orientations, and behaviors that officers, general managers, and employees already have. In interviewing a potential employee, managers need to recognize that he or she has these desirable attitudes, orientations, and behaviors. Otherwise managers will not hire the person because they believe that these characteristics are not trainable. As one employee states:

> So that's one thing that the manager looks for, our attitudes toward each other. Everybody has a bad day. . . . But if there is a *definite ongoing* problem, they either move you, or something has to happen if you can't get along. We work too close and too many hours to have somebody here like that. And that's something when we are interviewing, something I knew when I was doing the hiring I would spend about 20 minutes with each person just talking to them. You know, it's a lot easier to hire somebody for paperwork and train them than train them on their attitude. I felt that an attitude is more important than training the paperwork. Everybody can learn to write orders or whatever. They may be not as fast as others, but you *can learn.* But you can't retrain that attitude, if you don't have it. . . .
>
> I wanted to make sure that she was *really willing to do*—I told her that she wasn't hired just for the order desk, or just for whatever. She was hired to do whatever needed to be done. And I want to see that attitude. Of course, you can show that attitude but then after three months down the line, the newness is gone and the old attitude is gonna reappear. So I think a lot has to do with the right attitude, and a sense of humor. You really need a good sense of humor.

Or a vice president and former general manager explains:

I think 90% is what you are born with, 10% is developed. It's just something that's in your nature. You are born with it, maybe not born but by the time you are two or three years old, it's just an attitude that you have. You know, we have employees that come in who are extremely bright, but they don't have that attitude. And you can sense whether or not they can be the most effective employee, because some of them just don't have that. . . . So usually it clicks or it doesn't click.

You can talk about a qualification for a specific job and then you can see if somebody is qualified or not, their background and their attitude, and then you feel if they fit. And every organization has a type of person that fits. Our particular type of person is, we need to have people who are self-motivated, you know, initiators. We need to have people that are profit oriented. We need to have people that are communicators, people oriented, people that are willing to take responsibility.

A lot of companies are not structured like that. . . . They look for specific staff, task people where they become like human robots where you do this all day long. . . . There is no real meshing of all these skills or talents. . . . There is a different attitude that we have within our company. It's not a lot of real strong centralized control. Basically there are a lot of entrepreneurial skills out in the field that make our divisions click. You know, it's better to have all the superstars in the field than having all the superstars up in corporate and you just tell anybody out in the field what to do. That would never work for us.

Already possessing this "attitude," people are further developed through processes of coaching and role modeling, through some formal education outside the company if indicated, and through mentorship. New employees do not experience a formal introduction to BIND or to a particular division. Once hired they are encouraged to take their own initiative. Management expects that they will contribute their knowledge and skills and that they take responsibility for their own learning about BIND by asking people questions—both coworkers and superiors.

Management encourages employees to improve their education. Fees for work-related formal education are partially reimbursed if a class is completed with a C grade and fully reimbursed if the grade is B or better. Several employees have taken advantage of this opportunity in the past and still do, although the plant manager, a 72-year-old person who has been with the division since it was founded, felt that people should use it more often.

In addition management deliberately creates situations for people to learn new and different skills. Employees are moved within their divisions as well as across divisions. They are exposed to different tasks, situations, and information. When jobs open up at any level, BIND's employees have first priority. Only when a position cannot be filled from within will an outsider be hired. Especially in higher-level positions, management considers promotion from within important for two reasons: motivation and similar ways of thinking. The president explains:

> In an upper-level position I would think twice before I would go out and ask an outsider and go through the pain of getting him to think the way I would like him to think.

This orientation is rooted in the belief and practice of using cultural knowledge as a means of social control. This is a necessity for the functioning of this company with its loosely coupled divisions and its entrepreneurially oriented employees. Common emphases and directory knowledge of culture serve as invisible linkages between people in different locations. They guide them in their behavior and make them do the right things in their own way. As described by the president:

> I depend on . . . this culture . . . being passed along. I think over the years the selection of management, there is a management selection process, you keep all the people that are compatible with the way we are thinking, the corporate office and the division level, generally compatible. This is what we hope. It is, we gather around friends. I'm sure you gather with people who think and feel like

you do. It's the same way here in this company. I like to think that it's the reflection of the kind of people we have but I think we are.

Any number of times people would come in the company and visit with us sense the difference, that it's pervasive. It doesn't end with just the people you talk to but they find as they go through the company that there is a commonality, philosophically, in the business.

[By *commonality* he means] I think [the employees] know we are concerned about them, management. We like to think that we are a people-oriented company. And we sense that we have a divided responsibility . . . we are responsible to the employees as management and to the shareholders. . . . We try not to either favor the one or the other, or one at the expense of the other. . . . We have, certainly in the upper level, a lower turnover than most other companies.

Other information from interviews and demographic data support these presidential beliefs and hopes: 46 out of 52 respondents saw their professional future in the company; 36 of them wanted to make the company more effective, successful, and help it grow—they identify with BIND's major goal. Ten of them want to stay in one of the divisions and finally retire. Of the 52 respondents who had just been hired, 3 did not yet know, and 3 wanted to leave. One of them did not like the type of work, another preferred a position that was not available within the division, and another wanted to return to his home country after having been with the division for over 20 years.

Employees have, in general, long tenure, and turnover is low, except in one department in the PA division. Its manager had retired two years earlier and had not planned for a successor. His position could not be filled for about 18 months. A consultant was hired in the meantime on a part-time basis, but this arrangement did not work out. Further analysis suggests that the turnover in this department can be attributed to the lack of stable management and some unusual turbulence that occurred in that department during that time. Otherwise people with short tenure had just been hired to fill new positions because the division was growing.

These data about the axiomatic type of cultural knowledge elucidate not only the processes of culture formation and perpetuation but also the role of the founder and leader in these processes. I examine this role further in the following section.

THE ROLE OF THE FOUNDER AND LEADER IN DEVELOPING CULTURAL KNOWLEDGE

Several authors have attributed the creation of culture—implicitly or explicitly—to a firm's founder, and its perpetuation to its leader. In doing so they have rarely specified the processes by which this is accomplished.[1] In contrast some authors have even started to question the importance of founders and leaders in culture formation and perpetuation.[2]

Selznick,[3] one of the frequently cited sources in the management culture literature, states, for example, that an organization's distinctive character—or culture—is created through a process in which the leader infuses values. But he does not elaborate on how this process is accomplished. According to Schein,[4] the formation of culture begins with the foundation of a group. This group is created on the basis of initial consensus that the founder's idea is a good one. The group begins to act and brings in new members. Cultural assumptions, beliefs, and values are then taught to organizational members. This conception overlooks or underspecifies, however, two aspects. Initial consensus must be created first, and the process of perpetuating cultural knowledge is accomplished not only through mechanisms of social learning but also through deliberate selection and screening processes.

The findings of this study support, to some extent, the assertion that the founder is important in creating and perpetuating cultural knowledge. More specifically they demonstrate the processes of forming, perpetuating, and especially changing cultural knowledge. The personal beliefs of BIND's new president—the founder of the PC division—frame the range of possibilities for acceptable cultural knowledge to develop. His beliefs influence the metaphors that he and others use to explain events. And they have led to a change in the kinds of cultural knowledge that had existed before in BIND under its founder. To BIND'S new president, a very "democratic guy," the company seems to be a means to ends that are oriented toward self-sufficiency and humanistic concerns. Originally his interest was in creating a means to support his family. In this later role as president of a publicly held company, he is attempting both to satisfy stockholders and to create a secure workplace for BIND's employees. The metaphors he uses to describe his activities in the company were taken from gardening and housekeeping such as "pruning," "cutting," and "housecleaning."

But he had to negotiate his beliefs with the beliefs of others who had a major stake in the company—the other corporate officers who were also stockholders. As a result he had to make compromises and adjust his personal beliefs to the necessities of the business situation as perceived by the entire group. The president stated, for example, that he never wanted to do business with the government—a common practice within the industry of his original company. He wanted instead to succeed on his own. He still thinks that the divisions should not bid for government contracts. Because he is not the sole owner, he tolerates government contracts, however, when others want to go ahead for the growth of their division and hence for the company's growth. He also mentioned that he had to learn to look at people and their performance objectively. After his company was acquired by BIND, people were no longer just good people or friends but also employees who had to perform according to certain standards. If those standards were not reached by them after several attempts and negotiation, they had to go even if they were his "old buddies."

The findings of this study also indicate that cultural knowledge can be changed if the pressure to do so is strong enough. Faced with financial losses and a devaluation of the company's stock, a new president took over. He formed the "operations group," composed of other corporate officers, and changed the company's cultural knowledge base. In long discussions with the corporate officers, they changed the cultural knowledge— especially the axiomatic and directory knowledge—in a short period of time.[5] The realization and dissemination of these changes throughout the company, however, took several years. The new top management group established policies and reinforced their observations. They informed people in key positions and "educated" them about the important new cultural beliefs and knowledge, which were then reinforced in various ways. They systematically promoted people who held the desirable cultural knowledge into key positions. Those who would not change had to go. They sold entire companies that did not fit into BIND's new scenario. New firms were acquired that already had management compatible with BIND's new cultural knowledge.

Another aspect that has been neglected in the literature so far is the role that employees or "followers" play in the process of perpetuating cultural aspects. Founders and leaders represent only a small portion of cultural members—without followers they cannot make their contribution and we cannot speak of "leadership." In this particular company the nature of employees and the respective control processes emerged as the key variables in the processes of maintaining and perpetuating cultural knowledge. Employees are carefully screened at all hierarchic levels for those beliefs, attitudes, and behaviors that are considered important.

An additional manifestation and validation of this screening process is a certain kind of nepotism that could be observed in both the PC and the GA divisions. Acquaintances, friends, and family members are brought into the divisions at all different levels. On the shop floor several children of workers had been hired. They either stayed there or advanced into inspection and production control departments. One of the general managers hired his nephew as a salesman, and the mother of the current president still came into one division's office once a week to do filing. A previous production control manager brought in his best friend: The former one advanced to the general manager's position and finally to the position of a vice president while his friend succeeded him both times as production control manager and then as general manager.

This nepotism is a special kind of screening based on the belief that it is always better to know the potentials and shortcomings of an employee and work around them rather than start with unknowns. These screening procedures ensure that those beliefs, attitudes, and respective behaviors that are considered important are held by new employees. They are constantly reinforced through processes of role modeling, coaching, performance evaluation, and surveillance to avoid unintended drift. The president's major interest in this study was, for example, to see how deeply his beliefs could be traced at the divisional level.

SUMMARY

Analysis of the interview data has revealed an additional kind of knowledge that was not included in the initial conception of cultural knowledge: axiomatic knowledge, which consists of those assumptions that have influenced the formation and perpetuation of BIND and its cultural knowledge base. These assumptions have emerged from the personal beliefs and personal values of the new president. They were negotiated with the other corporate officers in BIND's major restructuring process, and they replaced the ones created by BIND's founder. Top management and especially those decision makers who were present during the restructuring process were identified as major carriers of this kind of cultural knowledge. People at lower levels were not cognization of these assumptions when probed but they acted upon them (see dictionary knowledge). This was due to the special screening and solitiation process. The boundaries of axiomatic knowledge can, therefore, be set at the top management level.

Assumptions in five different areas have influenced the process of formation in the company: assumptions about controlling the company and its business environment, assumptions about how to make money, assumptions in regard to organizational design, assumptions about corporate responsibilities, and assumptions about people.

I identified two processes that perpetuate this axiomatic knowledge: selection of people with the "right" attitude as well as informal coaching and mentorship. BIND's new president—founder of one of the divisions—was found to play a major role in these processes: He brought in his personal beliefs and values, he acted as a role model, coach, and mentor, and he created and used several kinds of symbolic rewards to reinforce desired actions and thoughts.

Overall the results of this study have led to some more general considerations in regard to cultural knowledge in organizational settings. I outline them in the next chapter, including some of the implications for the concept of culture in organizational settings.

NOTES

1. Among these authors are Deal and Kennedy (1982), Peters and Waterman (1982), Schein (1983), and Van de Ven (1983).

2. Phillips (1984) questions, for example, such an influence.

3. Selznick (1957).

4. Schein (1983).

5. The collected data gave me insights about changes in dictionary and recipe knowledge.

NINE

Cultural Knowledge in Organizations: A General Framework

This chapter takes some of the results out of the immediate context of the study and explores their contributions to a more general framework of cultural knowledge. Relevant content areas of cultural knowledge are discussed and integrated into a cultural knowledge map with the four kinds of cultural knowledge.

RELEVANT CONTENT AREAS OF CULTURAL KNOWLEDGE

The results of the study indicate that eight content areas are relevant for an understanding of the cultural knowledge in a company. These eight areas emerged in the analysis of dictionary, directory, and axiomatic knowledge.[1] They refer to commonly held beliefs[2] about an organization's purpose, its structure, strategy, organizational members, task accomplishment, adaptation and change, and relations among people as well as their learning mechanisms. Figure 9.1 synthesizes the findings.

Figure 9.1. Relevant Content Areas of Cultural Knowledge

The four framing parameters *organizational purpose, organizational members, organizational strategy,* and *organizational design* present a frame for the four processes. They determine the range of possibilities for the way tasks are accomplished, how people relate to each other, how they accomplish adaptation and change, and the way learning takes place within a certain cultural environment. They have a structural and a static nature.

Task accomplishment, people relations, adaptation/change, and *learning mechanisms* refer to organizational processes that are dynamic in nature. In Figure 9.1 the thick arrows show the major directions of influence, whereas the thin arrows indicate existing interactions and codetermination among the parameters.

The sets of beliefs about organizational purpose and organizational members can be considered the foundations of a cultural knowledge map. *Organizational purpose* refers to beliefs about the mission[3] or the major intended goal seen for the company. The parameter *organizational members* refers to an area of beliefs about human beings and their nature, needs, skills, and capacities. Both represent dialectical cornerstones. These beliefs define and shape an organization's structure and strategy as well as theories of action about the four organizational processes. The study revealed, for example, that the kind of people BIND considered desirable, those they wanted to keep and attract, required a structure that would allow them to enact their entrepreneurially oriented behavior. One could also imagine that the necessities of a given structure require people with certain preferences.

This knowledge delineates and determines the range of possible choices that are both available and acceptable for exploring structural and strategic parameters and organizational processes. These aspects of cultural knowledge are rather stable over time. Changes in beliefs about organizational members and the purpose of a specific organization may, nevertheless, occur. If they occur they are most likely based on dramatic events and will have a revolutionary rather than an evolutionary nature.

Beliefs about an organization's design and strategy are two additional pillars in determining boundaries for organizational processes. These sets of beliefs are, however, influenced and predetermined by beliefs and assumptions about the purpose of the company and about people. *Organizational structure* refers to formal aspects of organizational design such as job design, lines of responsibility, and means of coordination and control. Beliefs about *organizational design* refer to generalized plans for action that portray and prescribe the best ways to achieve an organization's major purpose.

Both parameters are interrelated with and codetermined by the three organizational processes. Once determined by beliefs about an organization's purpose and its members, they may be adjusted and shaped by changes in organizational processes. These beliefs are also rather stable over time; the nature of their change is, however, predominantly evolutionary and adaptive rather than revolutionary. This latter aspect distinguishes them from beliefs about organizational members and purposes.

Cognitions about the parameters of task accomplishments, people relations, adaptation/change, and learning mechanisms refer to beliefs about organizational processes. They have a dynamic rather than a static nature. Their rate of change in an organization is determined by the specific interpretation and enactment of the parameter adaptation/change.[4]

Beliefs about the process of *task accomplishment* depict organizational members' theories of action about how to achieve certain outcomes. These theories consist of directory knowledge that delineates means and causal relations about how to solve the problems of task accomplishment. In the case of decision making these beliefs specify who has to be involved, what kind of information is gathered, where it is obtained, and what kind of people make final decisions.

Beliefs about processes regarding *people relations* refer to organizational members' theories of action about how to relate to and interact with other people who are relevant to the organization. Relevant people are the company's stakeholders. They may be insiders such as employees at different levels; but they may also be outsiders such as customers, suppliers, competitors, or stockholders. This knowledge determines the degree of formality, the means, and the intensity in terms of relating with individuals. It specifies whether people are addressed by their first or last names and whether interactions are reduced to exchanges of necessary work-related information or whether these exchanges are extended to chats about private interests. They indicate whether people prefer to interact directly, face-to-face, or mainly indirectly by using telephones, memos, or other means of communication.

Beliefs about the structural process *adaptation/change* refer to organizational members' theories of action, to their knowledge about how to accomplish change. This set of beliefs describes how to adapt to changing conditions and demands that have emerged either from the organization's relevant outside environment or from its inside environment. These beliefs specify what has to be done if a new technology emerges within the company's industry or if an employee suggests a new way of accomplishing a certain task. They delineate the parameters when, how, where, and by whom adaptations and changes are introduced into the organization.

Beliefs about *learning mechanisms* concern ways of acquiring new knowledge and perpetuating existing knowledge. They represent theories of action about how to learn and how to disseminate the available knowledge. This set of beliefs delineates where to go to find new information, whether a trade journal, trade show, or conference. They indicate whether necessary information is generated internally or whether people with the desired knowledge are hired from the outside. They specify whether the maintenance and perpetuation of knowledge is achieved predominantly in informal day-to-day interactions on the job or in formalized socialization and training programs.

These eight parameters are empirically based. They have emerged in the process of analyzing and interpreting the gathered data, and they have proven useful in describing, understanding, and integrating the findings of the study. I consider them, therefore, to be relevant content areas of the company's cultural knowledge map. The extent to which they are applicable to other companies needs to be determined in future research. Their specific interpretation and enactment are likely to differ from company to company, from industry to industry, and from society to society. Future research needs to address questions such as under what conditions they differ, to what extent and in which ways they differ, how comprehensive they are in rendering a sufficient understanding of cultural aspects in a company, and what other areas might need to be included.

The eight content areas represent a useful framework for examining the cultural context in an organization, but they are not *the* dimensions of culture. Several authors who have written about culture seem to infer that culture in organizations consists of a certain set of dimensions. And, once discovered, these dimensions will reveal the culture in a given setting. The existing literature, however, makes it difficult to decide which set of dimensions are closest to this finite one.[5] Because the proposed dimensions are chosen or developed a priori on the basis of theoretical considerations, they may reveal more—or at least as much—about the author and his or her training than about the cultural dimensions.[6]

It seems that the complex phenomenon called "culture" contains a multitude of dimensions. And the specific cultural setting determines which dimensions are the most relevant ones, as indicated by the findings in regard to dictionary knowledge. This implies that information about what kind of dimensions are considered relevant is an important characteristic of a specific cultural setting. In addition, depending on the specific nature and purpose of an investigation, some dimensions may be more relevant than others. This has to be determined for each specific case without claims of comprehensiveness in covering all dimensions of culture.

THE CULTURAL KNOWLEDGE MAP

The eight content areas that have emerged from the data of this study are now integrated with the four kinds of cultural knowledge. Such an integration results in a cultural knowledge map that delineates the kinds as well as the content areas of a company's relevant cultural knowledge.

The model shown in Figure 9.2 can be used to gain an understanding of a company's cultural knowledge, to collect data for purposes of intervention, or as a framework to guide research efforts. For demonstration purposes I have rearranged the relevant content areas in this figure.

Dictionary knowledge is especially relevant in regard to the four content areas of organizational purpose, organizational members, organizational strategy, and organizational design. This knowledge, which refers to the aspect of *what*, can be obtained from top management as well as from secondary data sources.

Directory knowledge needs to be gathered about the areas of task accomplishment, people relations, adaptations/changes, and learning mechanisms. This information reveals *how* these processes are accomplished in a company. It should be collected at all hierarchic levels. For intervention purposes it may

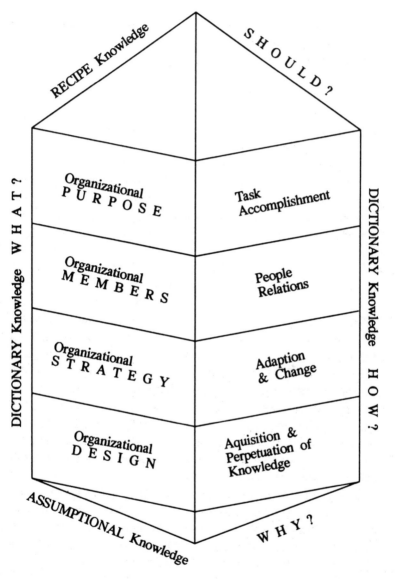

Figure 9.2. A Cultural Knowledge Map in Organizational Settings

be appropriate to choose one of the respective areas. Such a choice should, however, be guided by information collected previously and analyzed.

Recipe knowledge reveals ideas about desired changes or *should's*. Even though I obtained little information about this type of knowledge in the study, it is still worth pursuing in future research. The available data suggest that a comparison between recipe knowledge and directory knowledge may reveal important insights into the qualities of coordination and internal politics. A small amount of recipe knowledge consistent with directory knowledge may indicate a high degree of coordination, little internal politics, and high levels of performance. A large amount of recipe knowledge that differs from directory knowledge may indicate the opposite. To gain such insights a researcher needs to collect recipe knowledge from people throughout the company.

Axiomatic knowledge gives insight into the *why* behind information in the various content areas. This kind of knowledge is more difficult to obtain as it is predominantly held by long-tenured key decision makers such as the founder, long-standing president, vice presidents or turn around managers. Axiomatic knowledge is valuable for an evolutionary understanding of a company's cultural knowledge. Such an understanding may, however, not always be necessary for cultural interventions, especially if this knowledge dates back to several generations of organizational members. At BIND this axiomatic knowledge had developed 15 years prior to the study, and it could be obtained from the current president and vice presidents who were part of the company's major restructuring process at that time. Because organizational members had been selected on the basis of this cultural knowledge, they acted in alignment with it but were not cognizant of it.

Overall the findings of this study support the notion that culture in organizations is a multifaceted, multidimensional concept. Its cognitive component consists of four kinds of cultural knowledge and at least eight relevant content areas or dimensions. They can be selected and arranged in various sets depending on the specific purpose of a researcher or a practitioner. None of the sets is, however, comprehensive in describing all aspects of the cognitive component of culture in a specific organization. They characterize certain aspects of a cultural context that are considered relevant by the person who conducts the investigation.

The proposed model is, therefore, only one framework out of other possible conceptualizations that can be applied in gaining an understanding of the phenomenon of culture in organizational contexts. Based on the focus of the research and the state-of-the-art knowledge about culture in organizations, it represents—to the researcher at this point—the best choice for integrating and understanding the cultural knowledge base of the studied company. It has proven useful and comprehensive in capturing existing cultural knowledge and in gaining an understanding and appreciation of BIND's cultural context. I consider it applicable to other organizational contexts across industries.

The following chapter discusses more general insights from this study concerning the relationship between cultural knowledge, strategy, and organizational processes.

NOTES

1. Because of the relatively few data obtained about recipe knowledge when compared to the other three kinds of cultural knowledge, I have not explicitly included the recipe themes in these more general considerations.

2. The terms *assumptions, beliefs,* or *convictions* could be used synonymously in this context to refer to those cognitions that are commonly held based on emotions and not necessarily based on factual grounds.

3. The term *mission* is used by several authors to refer to the overarching, intangible goal of a company. At BIND *mission* had a rather pragmatic meaning. To better fit this pragmatic meaning, I chose the term *purpose* instead.

4. The recipe theme "Approach to Change" is related to adaptation/change; the recipe theme "acting vs. talking about acting" is related to "Task Accomplishment." The recipe theme "Problem Areas" could be added as a fifth organizational process. The recipe theme "Time Frame" could act as another framing parameter for the beliefs about organizational processes. This would support Schein's (1985) set of basic assumptions, which he adopted from Kluckhohn and Strodbeck (1961).

5. The different kinds of dimensions that can be found in the literature have been discussed in Chapter 2. Kluckhohn and Strodbeck (1961) differentiate five

dimensions of culture that have been introduced into the organizational literature by Schein (1983, 1984). Other dimensions are used by Kilmann and Saxton
(1983), Deal and Kennedy (1982), Lorsch and Lawrence (1965), Harrison (1972),
and Pümpin (1984).

6. Tichy's findings about consultants and the kinds of client problem they
consider relevant support this notion (Tichy, 1975). Hofstede (1980) discusses
this issue in regard to culture.

TEN

The Cultural Link Between Strategy and Organizational Processes

The previous chapters synthesized the major findings of the study in regard to relevant content areas of cultural knowledge. I also discussed the cultural knowledge map in which content areas are integrated with the different kinds of cultural knowledge. This chapter addresses the insights gained from the study about the relationship between cultural knowledge, strategy, and organizational processes.

In general claims have been made in the literature that strategy influences organizational culture and, conversely, that organizational culture influences strategy. More specifically strategists who take a rational point of view assert that a firm's culture needs to follow its strategy for best results. This assertion has been influenced by the notion that structure follows strategy.[1]

Before we go into further details of the relationship between strategy, organizational processes, and cultural knowledge, we need to have a basic understanding of strategy.

THE STRATEGY PERSPECTIVE

Strategy, like *culture*, has been defined in different ways. It can be described as a broad formula for the way a business is going to compete, what its goals should be, and what policies will be needed to carry out those goals.[2] Others see it as a pattern in streams of decisions[3] or as the causes that mold streams of decisions into patterns.[4] Many authors and practitioners consider strategic planning predominantly a rational activity based on quantitative methods. The overall aims of strategic planning are to identify opportunities, threats, and finally a unique product market niche for the firm.

The importance of culture for strategic concerns has only recently gained more interest in the strategy literature. This is, in part, due to the realization that strategic planning by itself often does not produce visible changes in a firm. Such changes that make a difference require organizational members who will carry through the strategic plans. In these endeavors they need to be supported by an appropriate structure and systems[5]. Some authors, therefore, advise those who are interested in strategy implementation to regard organizational culture as a concept of core interest.[6]

THE "BEST FIT" APPROACH AND ITS PROBLEMS

The above considerations have led to a "best fit" approach in strategic planning. The strategy and culture of a firm need to be aligned with each other.[7] One hopes that the risk of a failing implementation is thus reduced and that the expected outcomes will result. Within this "best fit" perspective, culture has been treated either as an obstacle or as an influencing variable. If culture is considered to be an obstacle, strategic planning and implementation of the plans usually take into consideration only those aspects of it that absolutely cannot be neglected. Basically culture is treated as a nuisance and plans are developed despite the existing culture. On the other hand, if culture is considered an influencing variable, managers can manipulate it, change it, or manage it according to the desired strategy. Both approaches are, however, based on a functionalistic and, therefore, reduced view of culture in organizations, which is rather limited in capturing the nature of complex human systems.[8]

THE CULTURAL KNOWLEDGE LINK

In addition strategists pay little attention to the fact that the perceptions and thoughts of managers may be influenced by a firm's cultural context. Some authors suggest, for example, a strong influence of cultural beliefs on the initiation of strategic change and on the perception that strategic change is necessary.[9] This influence may lead to systematic biases in perceiving and interpreting environmental opportunities and threats, which, in turn, may lead to different activities. Sapienza found such differences in her study of the decision-making processes of two different top management groups. Both dealt with the same environmental change: a deregulation of their industry. Her research shows that one group interpreted the change as an opportunity and developed opportunity-seeking actions. The other group interpreted the same event as a threat; this management group felt confined and reacted accordingly.

The study described here sheds more light on the nature of the influence between strategy, processes, and culture in organizations. More specifically I observed that cultural knowledge acts as a link between strategy and organizational processes. I found several reciprocal relationships between strategic issues and cultural knowledge, between cultural knowledge and organizational processes, and between organizational processes and strategic issues. The latter were mediated by cultural knowledge. These relationships may be influencing, guiding, and/or reinforcing in nature.

On the strategy side I found that cultural beliefs influence the formulation of strategic intentions, that they shape the realization of strategic intentions, and that they influence the maintenance process of realized strategic intentions as well as their reshaping. On the organizational process side I found that cultural beliefs guide and thus influence the specific enactment of organizational processes, which, in turn, reinforce cultural beliefs. I have indicated these reciprocal relationships in the previous chapter in Figure 9.2 without referring to their nature. This nature is now illustrated in Figure 10.1.

The results of the study indicate that existing cultural knowledge, strategy, and organizational processes began to be questioned when the top management group perceived threats in the internal and external environments of the firm. As a first step they debated and negotiated axiomatic knowledge. Once in place this axiomatic knowledge defined the firm's purpose, its strategic intention, its design, and characteristics of preferred members. These basic beliefs then guided their strategic decisions about retaining and selling existing firms or divisions and about acquiring new firms. In addition these basic beliefs guided their decisions and actions in regard to organizational processes. In particular their basic beliefs about preferred organizational members and the subsequent decision about the required structure set the stage for the specific enactment of organizational processes.

In the process of negotiating axiomatic knowledge, existing dictionary and directory knowledge was altered. This knowledge then guided the thoughts, attention, and actions of organizational members both in terms of organizational processes and in terms of strategic concerns and their implementation. Their actions, and the outcomes of their actions, in turn, maintained, reinforced, and further adjusted directory, dictionary, and axiomatic knowledge. I will now illustrate these processes in regard to the specific findings of the study.

THE DEVELOPMENT OF STRATEGIC INTENTIONS

When faced with perceived threats in the internal and external environments of the firm, the new top management group developed and negotiated their axiomatic knowledge base. Externally the value of the firm's stock had started to decline.

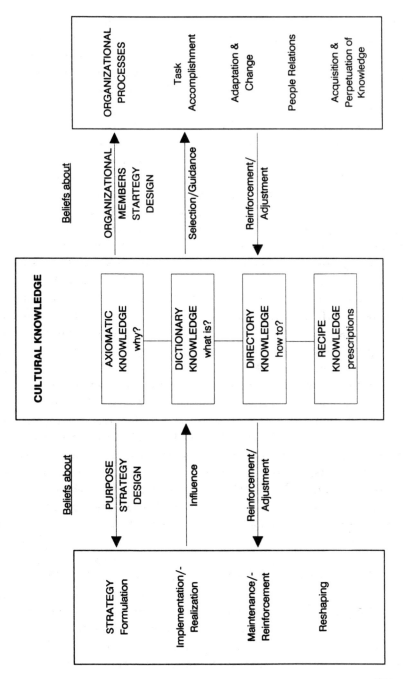

Figure 10.1. The Relationship Between Cultural Knowledge, Strategy, and Organizational Processes

157

Internally rapid growth through acquisitions had created major problems of integration, coordination, and management. Within four years the number of employees had grown from 70 to 1,500. The new top management group started to question their existing strategy, structure, and management approach. They negotiated some fundamental beliefs concerning BIND's purpose, strategy, structure, and organizational members. The formulation of these beliefs were influenced by their own— positive and negative—experiences, that is, their already established cultural knowledge that consists of axiomatic, dictionary, directory, and recipe knowledge.

Once this group of people had agreed on their fundamental beliefs—that is, axiomatic knowledge—these beliefs influenced their choices with regard to strategy, structure, management systems, and organizational members. Their beliefs about BIND's purpose and strategic intentions helped them regroup the acquired firms and decide which ones to sell, which ones to keep, and which ones to acquire. In turn these decisions had a reinforcing effect on the belief structure.

Their basic beliefs about organizational members—the kind of qualities they appreciated in people and whom they wanted to keep in BIND—made them change the firm's structure. The intention of the prior president was to have a highly centralized organizational design. The new group decided that a decentralized structure would better fit their preferred type of organizational member as well as their own capabilities. Each member of the top management group had in-depth knowledge of one industry and market. But, due to their position, they had lost direct relationships with customers and hence a feel for customers' needs and desires. In terms of organizational members they wanted to retain and attract entrepreneurially oriented people who assume responsibility and who are eager to seize opportunities.

REALIZING STRATEGIC INTENTIONS

They used five major processes to realize their strategic intentions and to maintain them. All of them deal with human resource management. These influence the range of acceptable actions within BIND. The top management group tried to retain those employees who fit their desired image. They carefully prescreened new employees for the qualities that they appreciated. They developed employees with perceived potential. They considered themselves and each person with managerial responsibilities as a role model of the new cultural reality. They mentored people in key positions. And they designed organizational systems to facilitate and reinforce the new strategies. These included the organizational structure, reward systems, communication, and management information systems.

The preselected and "molded" organizational members then created, enacted, and hence shaped organizational processes in BIND. The way tasks are accomplished, the way people interact with each other, the way they adapt collectively to changes, and the way they acquire and perpetuate knowledge depend on these very people. While axiomatic knowledge guided and influenced the selection of organizational members at all hierarchic levels, once hired, the members' choice of actions was invisibly guided by dictionary, directory, and recipe knowledge.

REINFORCING, ADJUSTING, AND
RESHAPING STRATEGIC INTENTIONS

Subsequently their actions further reinforced existing cultural knowledge, added to it, and adjusted it to some extent. These adjustments occurred on the basis of action outcomes. Once they had learned their group's dictionary knowledge, it told them what to look for, where to pay attention, how to set priorities. The acquired directory knowledge served as an invisible guide for their behaviors. It told them how to work and how to interact with their bosses, their colleagues, their subordinates, and with outsiders. The accumulating experience further reinforced and adjusted to some extent their actions and the guiding cultural knowledge.

Thus organizational processes that are invisibly guided by cultural knowledge and enacted by organizational members realize the formulated strategic intentions, reinforce them, and adjust them according to growing experience. The ways in which organizational members accomplished their tasks, adapted to changing conditions, related to people, and acquired and perpetuated knowledge helped realize and maintain the strategic intentions formulated by the top management group. Organizational members acted within the framework of cultural knowledge and made the retained divisions perform according to the established standards. If these standards were not met, a vice president would point it out and advise the divisions on further actions.

The accumulating experience of successes and failures guided them in reshaping their strategic intentions. On one occasion, for example, their belief "small is better than big" was seriously tested. One of BIND's divisions was extremely successful and grew from about 100 employees to 480 within a couple of years. With this growth they suddenly encountered several managerial problems that reinforced and amplified their belief that the size of BIND's divisions should not exceed approximately 100 employees. The top management group had to realize that their managerial preferences did not work successfully in larger divisions. They finally decided to reduce the division to its original size.

Because little information was obtained about recipe knowledge, I can only speculate that recipes of success and failure emerge from accumulating experience. Actions that have worked well are gathered in the form of recipes of success. They are most likely to be repeated in the future. Those actions that have produced failures are accumulated as recipes of failure and avoided in future actions. These recipes of success and failure may lead to prescriptions and "should's" in the form of recipe knowledge.

NEW INSIGHTS ABOUT THE RELATIONSHIP
BETWEEN STRATEGY AND CULTURE

Findings about the relationship between cultural knowledge, strategy, and organizational processes support and further specify assertions by other authors. They clearly support Donaldson and Lorsch's argument that strategic change requires a basic rethinking of the beliefs by which a company defines and carries on its business.[10] At BIND these basic beliefs were not, however, developed over many years, as these authors have suggested. It took the new top management group less than a year to develop and negotiate their cultural beliefs.

Once a need had been perceived for strategic change and their cultural belief system was negotiated, these influenced top management's perception and interpretation of the internal and external environments, which was suggested by the other authors.[11] Schein suggests, for example, a reciprocal influence between strategic issues and culture. Initially the environment influences the formation of culture. But, once culture is present in the sense of shared assumptions, those assumptions influence the perception and definition of environmental factors considered relevant. And Homans has argued that the external system, which is composed of physical, technical, and sociocultural factors, generates activities and interactions among the members of a group. These interactions generate sentiments and norms—or a group culture—that influence the group's activities once established.[12]

Once in place this cultural knowledge influenced not only the strategic issues but also their implementation, more specifically their realization, maintenance, and reshaping.[13] An important finding is the interlocking use of different managerial "tools" to realize and maintain the newly developed cultural beliefs and strategic intentions. These were pervasive in different aspects of human resource management, in the behavior of managers, in newly developed managerial systems, and in control functions. Over the years the newly developed and reshaped strategic intentions became translated into daily work behaviors, thus reinforcing BIND's cultural knowledge. This suggests a reciprocal relationship between cultural knowledge, strategic issues, and organizational processes.

SUGGESTIONS FOR STRATEGY FORMULATION AND IMPLEMENTATION

These insights indicate the difficulties involved in introducing and achieving noticeable changes both in a firm's strategic direction and in its cultural context. A new strategic orientation needs to be supported or initiated by changes in the cultural knowledge base, which, in turn, requires changes in organizational processes. In terms of strategy formulation, two approaches seem most appropriate:

- a combined approach between insiders and outsiders in which different perspectives are applied or
- a dialectical approach by insiders in which cultural knowledge is constantly scrutinized to increase awareness of existing biases.[14]

In terms of strategy implementation, the findings suggest that the kind of people as well as the structure and systems that support them in their activities are crucial in realizing strategic intentions within a supportive cultural setting. Hence three major issues need to be considered in implementing strategic issues:

- deliberate choice/preselection of organizational members who fit the intended strategy,
- training and socialization programs that develop organizational members toward the intended strategy, and
- (re)design of managerial systems that support the thoughts and actions of organizational members in terms of realizing the strategic intentions.

The next chapter summarizes the major points of this study and draws some conclusions about the nature of culture in organizational settings.

NOTES

1. Proponents of the idea that "structure follows strategy" are, for example, Chandler (1962), Justis, Judd, and Stephens (1985), Kobi and Wüthrich (1986), and Porter (1980).

2. Porter (1980).

3. Miller and Mintzberg (1974).

4. Hedberg and Jönsson (1977).

5. Lenz (1985) discusses the problem of overplanning, and Ansoff (1979) addresses the importance of implementation.

6. See, for example, Gupta and Stengrevics (1983).

7. This "best fit" approach between organizational strategy and culture can be found, for example, in the work of Pascale and Athos (1981), Peters and Waterman (1982), and Schwartz and Davis (1981).

8. Sackmann (1990) discusses the different perspectives of culture in organizations and addresses the problems associated with the treatment of culture as a variable.

9. See, for example, Dutton and Duncan (1987a, 1987b).

10. Donaldson and Lorsch (1983).

11. See, for example, Sapienza (1985) or Schein (1985).

12. Homans (1950).

13. Lorsch (1985) and Gupta and Stengrevics (1983) suggest, for example, that cultural beliefs also influence strategy implementation.

14. Mason (1969), Mitroff, Emshoff, and Kilmann (1979), and Mason and Mitroff (1981) have already suggested such a dialectical approach to strategic planning.

ELEVEN

Conclusions on the Nature and Concept of Culture in Organizational Settings

This chapter summarizes the major issues of this work including the rationale underlying the study, the conceptualization of culture in terms of cultural knowledge and the research findings. In addition, the chapter outlines and assesses the major contribution of this work with its implications for organizational design.

WHY CULTURAL KNOWLEDGE?

This work represents an exploratory study of culture in organizational settings. I have argued that several assumptions are held about culture that were imported predominantly and selectively from the concept's anthropological roots. In this process of concept displacement, underlying assumptions were not examined if they were also appropriate in organizational settings. Rather than debating opinions that are partially based on untested assumptions, I argued that there was a need for more empirically generated knowledge. In a review of relevant literature, I identified three different foci in regard to culture in organizational settings: a holistic one, a variable one, and a cognitive one. I pointed out that the holistic perspective does not lend itself to empirical research and that no distinctions are made between structural and developmental aspects of culture. The manifestation-oriented perspective needs to be supplemented by the cognitive perspective if one wants to understand the special meanings that individuals attribute to manifestations in a given cultural setting. For these reasons this study has focused on the cognitive components of culture that I have defined both from a structural and from a developmental perspective.

Because there is no agreement in the literature about what the relevant components of culture in organizations are, and because concepts such as philosophies, values, norms, ideology, or beliefs have been used imprecisely, I developed a structural framework of cultural knowledge. The proposed framework is based on generic characteristics of the social construction of reality or everyday theory. Originally I differentiated three kinds of cultural knowledge: dictionary, directory, and recipe knowledge. Dictionary knowledge consists of commonly held cognitions about "what is" in a company; it is descriptive in nature. Directory knowledge consists of commonly held cognitions about the aspect of "how" in a company; it is causal in nature and refers to processes. Recipe knowledge consists of commonly held cognitions about improvements or repair strategies, the "should's" in a firm; it is normative and prescriptive in nature. The analyses and interpretation of the data suggested that a fourth kind of cultural needs to be included: axiomatic knowledge. Axiomatic knowledge asks "why"; it contains the ultimate assumptions that exist in a firm, which cannot further be reduced.

CONTRIBUTIONS OF THE STUDY

I designed the study so that we could gain a better understanding of culture in organizational settings. The proposed framework of cultural knowledge served as a broad orientation during the interview process. It was applied, among other frameworks, in the analysis of the interview data. The resulting data were validated with observational and secondary data.

The overall results of the study make several methodological and theoretical contributions, which have implications for practice. In general the developed methodology was suitable for the purpose of the study. It was comprehensive and unobtrusive in surfacing cultural knowledge and in gaining insights into the nature of culture in organizational settings. I discuss its specific contributions in more detail at the end of Appendix A: Methodology.

In terms of theory the results of this study make five contributions. They suggest that culture in organizations needs to be conceptualized in more complex ways. The findings indicate the scope and locations of cultural groupings. They support the proposed theoretical model of cultural knowledge in organizations and specify it further. They suggest structural components and relevant content areas of cultural knowledge, and they specify processes of culture formation, perpetuation, and change including the roles of the founder and leader in these processes.

Despite the selective focus on ideational or cognitive components of culture, the study has shown that culture in organizational settings is quite complex in terms of its structure, dynamics, and content. Up to now authors have argued exclusively for either a homogeneous nature of culture or a heterogeneous nature. This study indicates that, at the same time, culture may have a homogeneous quality as well as a heterogeneous one. By differentiating the kinds of cultural knowledge, a homogeneous quality of culture or cultural synergy emerged in regard to directory knowledge, whereas several cultural groupings emerged in regard to dictionary knowledge, and a different grouping surfaced in regard to axiomatic knowledge.

The results of the study provide further insights into the boundaries of cultural groupings, and their grouping mechanisms, in terms of the different kinds of cultural knowledge. In this particular company functional domain emerged as an important grouping factor in regard to dictionary, recipe, and axiomatic knowledge. The functional domain has an active nature. It relates to a person's perceived responsibility rather than to a firm's prescribed functions.

The results also suggest factors that help maintain existing cultural groupings and their cultural knowledge. Depending on the kind of cultural knowledge, a combination of different factors are used, such as organizational design, selection procedures, incentive and reward systems, organizational control mechanisms as well as employee development in terms of role modeling and mentoring. Furthermore the study identified variables that influence the content of cultural groupings and their knowledge. Here again different ones may apply in regard to the different kinds of cultural knowledge. While the specific nature of employees and the beliefs and experience of the new president and corporate officers are both influencing factors in regard to dictionary knowledge, only the latter influences axiomatic knowledge. Divisional boundaries, the nature of work, and hierarchic levels shape the content of cultural groupings and their knowledge in terms of dictionary knowledge, whereas the specific nature of employees and hierarchic levels seem to operate in regard to recipe knowledge.

The proposed model of dictionary, directory, and recipe knowledge turned out to be useful in understanding the cultural knowledge base of the company under investigation. Based on the various analyses of the collected data, the originally proposed framework of cultural knowledge was complemented by axiomatic knowledge, which gives insights into the "why" of things in a given cultural setting.

ASSESSMENT AND CONCLUSION

How does this framework differ from existing conceptualizations of culture in organizations? When compared with existing conceptualizations, I see four major advantages of the developed framework of cultural knowledge. It is both more comprehensive and more specific, it combines structural aspects with historic and dynamic ones, and it can be studied.[1] Existing conceptions of culture have predominantly focused on assumptions, values, norms, and/or beliefs. None of these concepts has been explored sufficiently yet. Only norms, and to some extent assumptions, have been implemented.[2] Furthermore none of these concepts alone can tap all the different aspects of culture in an organization. Their selective focus may be sufficient for a specific purpose but it is hypocrisy to then claim that one specific concept represents *the* culture of an organization.

The most important and the most emphasized aspects of dictionary knowledge within a given organization come close to the concept of values—those things are considered important and which are valued. They represent those collectively held aspects of "what is" that are collectively emphasized. This does not, however, preclude less emphasized aspects from being cultural. Depending on the purpose of an investigation, those less emphasized aspects may also reveal important specifications of cultural aspects in that organization.

Norms are related to recipe knowledge in regard to their "ought to" nature and to directory knowledge as far as it reflects rules of behavior. In contrast to norms, directory knowledge refers to actual knowledge of past and current behaviors and to ideas of how things have been and are being done—not how they should be done. As the findings of the study indicate, directory knowledge may finally lead to guidelines or even to rules of behavior that are then applied in future activities. Guidelines have a less mandatory nature for behavior than rules. While guidelines were prevalent in the researched company, it is very likely that other organizations—for example, bureaucracies—are full of overspecified rules for behavior. These may become dysfunctional when narrowly observed and held regardless of outside demands.

Axiomatic knowledge refers to the presumptions or axioms that were negotiated in the creation or restructuring phase of the company. Axiomatic knowledge is related to assumptions as specified in Schein's work.[3] In contrast to his work axiomatic knowledge here, however, is only considered to be one aspect of the cultural knowledge base. It is not the essence of culture or even its most important component. The study further suggests that information about axiomatic knowledge is important if one is interested in the formation of cultural knowledge, its origins and reasons for existence. In this particular study axiomatic knowledge could only be generated from those people who were key decision makers in the restructuring process of BIND several years earlier. The other members of BIND functioned as full members of the cultural setting without knowing about existing axiomatic knowledge. They behaved within the framework of these assumptions but they were not aware of them, despite further probing. It is, therefore, questionable whether one needs to know axiomatic knowledge or the basic assumptions of a firm to gain an understanding of a specific cultural setting. The assumptions may have surpassed their founding members or those people who have introduced a major restructuring. This is, for example, the case in a bureaucracy, where roles and positions are depersonified to a high degree.[4]

I have defined cultural knowledge as being composed of different types of cognitions. These are constructs taken from cognitive psychology consisting of sets of categories that guide perception and thinking.[5] I used the term *cognition* so as to set preconceptions aside until empirical evidence might be available. Based on the findings of this study, I suggest replacing the term *cognition* with the better known words *belief* or *idea*. The different kinds of cultural knowledge are composed of various beliefs or ideas that may be grounded in prior experiences, in vicarious experiences, in factual data, or in pure assumptions without any factual support. Over time they are assigned with different degrees of importance and held with different emotional investment. *Belief* in this context is hence a much broader term than in the common definition of *culture* as "a set of values, beliefs and norms."

Another advantage of the proposed conception lies in its integration of structural aspects of cultural dynamics, complexities, and even paradoxes. Prior conceptions of culture have either postulated one monolithic entity or several subcultures. The findings of this study show that cultural groupings can form differently in terms of the various kinds of knowledge. They indicate that monolithic aspects can be combined with subcultural differentiation within the same company. The specific findings obtained in this study about cultural groupings and cultural synergism in regard to the respective cultural knowledge seem to be ideal for high organizational performance.

IMPLICATIONS FOR ORGANIZATION DESIGN

More generally these findings have important implications for designing organizations, for designing organizational control mechanisms, for analyzing the nature and quality of a company's internal integration, and for designing and recommending changes. Functional domain or perceived responsibilities could become the basic building block in designing new organizations or redefining existing ones. In regard to dictionary knowledge, cultural groupings other than functional domain groupings may indicate long-term performance problems. These may be due to internal politics or to the phenomenon called "group think."[6] A lack of cultural synergism at the directory level of cultural knowledge may indicate problems of integration and coordination since members of the same organization do not adhere to the same process. Cultural synergism in regard to this cultural knowledge can, therefore, also be considered to be a functional imperative for high levels of performance.

In the conception of cultural knowledge that I have presented here, internal politics may foster groupings according to perceived centers of power and/or according to dominant and emerging coalitions. Group think may also foster cultural groupings according to centers of power and influence. I have chosen a different approach to culture in organizational settings. This approach breaks with the traditional static conceptions in which culture has been equated with one or with several other ill-defined concepts. Nevertheless the usefulness of the presented conception should be further examined in future applications within different organizational settings.

The following chapter outlines some directions for future research.

NOTES

1. In technical terms the framework of cultural knowledge can be implemented.

2. Kilmann and Saxton (1983) developed a questionnaire to study cultural norms. Hofstede (1980) designed a questionnaire to investigate cultural values. Phillips (1990) used a modified version of the ethnographic interview to surface assumptions in her study of the fine arts museum and winery industries.

3. Schein (1985) considers assumptions to be the essence of culture. They are located at the deepest level of his framework.

4. Weber (1946) discusses the characteristics of bureaucracies.

5. See, for example, Foa and Foa (1974) and Schank and Abelson (1977).

6. Janis (1972) conducted research on the phenomenon of group think and describes its various characteristics.

TWELVE

Where Do We Go from Here?

This chapter discusses some directions for future research and implications for gaining an understanding of cultural settings.

The findings presented above have come from an exploratory study using a methodology that has strengths but also limitations. Based on an evaluation of the existing literature, as well as the lack of empirical knowledge about the concept of culture applied to organizational settings, I have argued that the most fruitful approach to research is a heuristic one. Such an inductive approach aims at discovery rather than explanations, and the generated information is relevant in its immediate context. Instead of imposing the researcher's preconceptions about what kind of information is important to collect to learn about the company's cultural knowledge, I derived concepts inductively from the accounts of organizational members. I analyzed and synthesized this insider knowledge and finally translated it. In this translation process I attempted both to reflect the essence of the cultural knowledge that is considered important by members of the research site and, at the same time, to make sense to the research community.

I chose a phenomenological approach to arrive at an insider's perspective and to learn to see and understand a part of employees' work lives from their frame of reference rather than my own. I used a simple but powerful test to confirm whether I could actually take the insider's perspective. This test consisted of mentally filling in gaps and anticipating the respondents' answers during the interviews. It is a variation of existing projective devices that have been used in cognitive research such as the Sentence Completion Test.[1] During interviews I formulated a question that I answered for myself on the basis of the given information before the answer was actually given by the respondent. A comparison of the explicitly given and implicitly formulated answers indicated whether and how well the respondent's perspective could be taken.

To ensure objectivity in this apparently subjective research process, the interviews were reanalyzed several times, in intervals of several weeks, for underlying themes. I critically discussed the emerging results on an ongoing basis with two colleagues who were informed yet not directly involved in the study. In addition each one of us had different professional training as well as cultural background. One used a strategic-Jamaican/North American lens, the other a policy-North American lens, and the researcher an organizational behavior-German/American lens. Once categories were developed I reapplied them to the original interview data until the best fitting set of categories had emerged.

I also used a triangulation approach[2] to ensure the validity of the data. Data were collected from different sources of information. I compared and contrasted these different types of information with each other and, in the case of divergence, I collected additional data to explore the variations.

For these reasons I consider the findings to be valid and objective. Due to the case study methodology, their range of validity is, however, restricted to the specific nature of the company that I studied and to the method I used for eliciting cognitions.

The study can answer several questions about the nature of culture and cultural knowledge in organizational settings. But it also generates many new questions that may be explored in future research.

SOME DIRECTIONS FOR FUTURE RESEARCH

Based on this study several directions can be taken in future research to generate further empirical knowledge about the concept of culture in organizational settings and to answer the questions that have emerged from this study. These directions point to research on both macro and micro levels of organizations as well as to investigations with a focus on methodology.

In general possibilities for the further development of frameworks for understanding cultural issues in organizations include different foci on specific aspects of culture. These need to be combined with considerations of alternative formats and different settings for eliciting, collecting, and analyzing data. Such approaches include the use of larger sample sizes and different research paradigms to determine the extent to which the reported findings are applicable to other companies within the same industry, to companies within different industries, and, finally, to companies within different regions and societies or nations.

More specifically the same research methodology can be taken to the next step and applied to another company from the same industry. A comparison between the findings would further validate and/or refine the theoretical conceptions developed here. Based on these results a research method needs to be developed that can be applied in comparative studies using larger sample sizes that include several companies from several industries and, finally, from several regions and nations. The results of such larger-scale studies could differentiate between cultural knowledge that pertains to an organization, to a specific industry, to a region, or to a nation.

On a micro-organizational level, future research can address several issues to further explore, specify, and validate the nature of cultural groupings within different organizational contexts. This includes a further investigation of the role of reward and control systems, organizational design, and internal politics in shaping and maintaining cultural groupings. The proposed conception of cultural knowledge also needs further validation in different contexts. And different issues should be used to elicit cultural cognitions.

The issue of innovation and its further specification in the form of changes that took place in the company proved to be a useful projective device to elicit cognitions and to gather beliefs and knowledge from organizational members. The question may arise as to whether the use of a different issue would have led to the same or similar data in regard to all or some levels of cultural knowledge. Different issues may also unravel different kinds of cognitions and knowledge. Based on theoretical considerations as well as on the data analyses, it seems that dictionary knowledge is more closely related to the chosen issue than directory, recipe, or axiomatic knowledge. The latter one appears to have more universal qualities of why, how, and how things are done better in the company regardless of the issue in focus. A comparison between the kind of information obtained with different issues may indicate to what extent the data are issue specific rather than universal for a company's cultural knowledge. Appendix B lists some specific questions that may be investigated in future research.

Another worthwhile pursuit is the development of a taxonomy or data base of cultural knowledge profiles obtained from sets of companies that operate under different legal conditions and in different industrial, geographic, social, and political environments. Emerging profiles can then be related to short-term as well as long-term behavioral and financial performance indicators. Detailed comparisons and contrasts across each single parameter as well as across different profiles may generate a differentiated understanding about the degree of functionality and effectiveness of certain cultural knowledge and specify the respective contexts. Conditions for the highest and lowest degrees of short- and long-term effectiveness may surface for different cultural contexts. Such a taxonomy or contingency information could eventually be used as a guideline for designing organizations and for improving existing ones.

IMPLICATIONS FOR UNDERSTANDING CULTURAL SETTINGS

Each intervention in the cultural context of a firm requires an understanding of that cultural context—be it to better understand a given cultural context, to emphasize its strengths, or to manage in a culture-aware fashion.[3] The findings of this study have implications for gaining such an understanding. For a general analysis of cultural context, I recommend the use of the term *change* as a device to elicit to cultural knowledge, because this term was generally understood by employees at all hierarchic levels. Furthermore the use of the term *change* allows respondents to reflect on a situation in which cultural habits were broken and hence become more visible.

The findings also suggest that three foci are important in the process of data collection that address the different kinds and content areas of cultural knowledge. The three foci are the specific emphases placed in the different kinds of cultural knowledge and their content areas, intentions and their realizations, and hierarchic levels.

The aspect of *emphasis* refers to the degree of importance placed on dictionary, directory, and recipe knowledge. Emphasis is related to the process of valuing and prioritizing perceived alternatives. As mentioned above the various emphases placed across different kinds of knowledge are important. Comparisons with the company's intended long-term strategy and with industry leaders will reveal strengths and weaknesses. Such comparisons may show the degree of adaptiveness of a company's cultural knowledge to the external environment and its specific requirements.

The aspect of *intention* refers to desired descriptions, processes, and prescriptions. It represents the design aspect of behaviors but not the behavior itself. Intentions indicate a disposition for behavior but not necessarily its realization.

The aspect of *realization* refers to realized descriptions, operations, and prescriptions. It represents enactments of intentions or felt implications of an enacted design. Realizations can also be considered the complementary side of intentions.

Realizations render intentions visible and demonstrate their impact or implications.

For a comprehensive and detailed understanding of a specific cultural setting, the emphases placed on cultural knowledge—especially on directory knowledge—need to be collected from organizational members across all hierarchic levels, not only from top management. Such a comprehensive analysis will reveal the cultural strengths and weaknesses of a company. A companywide comparison of this information indicates the degree of integration among the members of an organization. It may display problems of communication, decision making, coordination, or organizational control. It may uncover why certain products or processes do not turn out the way they were intended. If, within the same company, different emphases are placed in one of the content areas, the most likely results will be misunderstandings, friction, wasting of energy and resources as well as loss in quality. The nature of existing differences in emphases, therefore, need to be closely examined and used as a basis for designing appropriate interventions to reduce existing differences.

A comparison of intentions collected at the level of top management with specific realizations at different hierarchic levels will reveal the degree and locations of potential goal displacements. Due to an organization's division of labor, groupings with a major focus on design—such as top management—and with a major focus on the execution of these designs—such as production—may become isolated from each other over time. Members of the top management of a company may, for example, believe that all their intentions are being realized at lower levels in the company. This may, however, not be the case.

A comparison of the intentions and realizations in a given content area, such as the intention and realization of a specific strategy, indicates the specific areas and locations of drifting realizations and the degree of goal displacement. Researchers and managers alike can use this information to reexamine the respective intentions and their enacted realizations and to design corrective interventions to stop and reverse the drift.

The findings of this study suggest that the respective information should be obtained from different sources and locations within an organization. Intentions expressed in regard to content areas can be found at the level of top management and, to some extent, upper-middle management. Realizations of intentions should be collected at all levels of an organization, especially middle- and lower-level positions, whereas the aspect of implication dominates at a lower hierarchic level. An assessment of the emphasis on dictionary, directory, and recipe knowledge needs to be gathered from all levels of an organization as the emphasis may vary according to cultural groupings—in this study in regard to functional domains. Axiomatic knowledge, on the other hand, only seems to be available from the founder(s)/leader and "reshapers" who were involved in the founding process or in the most recent major restructuring process of a company.

Suggesting such companywide or specially focused data collection contradicts some current beliefs and practices in organizational research in which information about cultural aspects is gathered exclusively from top management.[4] Such a selective focus precludes the possibility that top management may be isolated at the top and dissociated from the lower operating levels. An analysis of axiomatic knowledge may, however, be important in several cases: if a major reorientation seems necessary in a company's cultural knowledge and in its respective practices, if the founder is still active and influential, or if the company had a dominant president of long tenure.

A last remark seems to be appropriate regarding the role of a researcher or change agent in the process of designing and implementing interventions in the cultural context. While it seems almost impossible to study and analyze the cultural context of a company without the assistance of an outsider's perspective, the design and implementation of interventions should be in the control of the organization's members. Based on the gathered information, outsiders can make recommendations for more or less appropriate interventions given that they are knowledgeable about the company's cultural context and about relevant external conditions. But outsiders will never have the leverage, persistence, time commitment, and degree of ownership necessary for carrying forth interventions that go to the essence of a company. In regard to the cultural context, the role of an outsider can be described as devil's advocate. Outsiders are important to help sustain the process of constant "culture care," to identify unintended drifts, to confront insiders with their basic beliefs and with the subtle enveloping processes of enculturation within the organization. Such an activity was expressed by one of the vice presidents at BIND as follows:

> Try to keep everybody open to new ideas . . . people get used of doing their job, maybe they are doing it in a certain way, and a lot of times they are getting locked in being maintainers rather than initiators or innovators. So every once in a while we have to go in and crack a portion of their brains, open it up for a while and air it out, get them to think about some new ideas.

NOTES

1. See Schroder, Driver, and Streufert (1967).
2. Webb, Campbell, Schwartz, and Sechrest (1966).
3. Sackmann (1990) differentiates, discusses, and describes different approaches to intervene in the cultural context of an organization.
4. See, for example, Davis (1984), Schein (1983), or Sethia (1983).

APPENDIX A

Methodology

The problem with the study of cultural knowledge is that this knowledge is difficult to identify and to decipher because its carriers take it for granted. Cultural knowledge is used habitually and goes unnoticed unless challenged. Culture in organizations has been studied in various ways depending upon the specific interests of the researcher. Approaches range from longitudinal ethnographic studies with a predominant focus on observations to in-depth interview methodologies and one-shot questionnaire approaches.

The objectives in designing an appropriate methodology for this study were to strike a balance between an extensive ethnography and a pragmatic instrumentation approach. Ethnographies as practiced in the field of anthropology are expensive in terms of man-hours. They yield a vast amount of rich and valuable data, but not all of it may be necessary to understand the cultural context of an organization, which differs from a societal context. A questionnaire approach, on the other hand, was considered inappropriate. Due to the lack of empirical knowledge about culture in organizations, such a deductive approach would require many assumptions made by the researcher. Based on evaluation of the existing literature and the lack of empirical knowledge, I felt that, at this point, only an inductive or heuristic approach could answer the questions posed in a satisfactory way.[1]

I established three criteria in developing a methodology for the study. It should consist of methods appropriate to elicit cognitive components of culture and to arrive at groupings of people holding similar cognitions. Because cognitions are individually held, data would have to be collected from individuals and then aggregated to a group level. More specifically the methodology should

(1) surface tacit components from the insiders' perspective,
(2) be sensitive to structural specifics such as subcultures, and
(3) enable comparisons across individuals and research sites.

These criteria led to the choice of a *design of successive comparisons* and to the development of an *issue-focused interviewing technique* as a focal method for data collection that was based on a *phenomenological orientation*. All interviews were tape-recorded, transcribed verbatim, and content analyzed using a theoretical content analysis. I used additional data sources (observations and documentary analysis) and a discussion of the results with top management for validation. Critical discussions with two colleagues ensured objectivity in the analysis and interpretation of the data.

AN ISSUE-FOCUSED INVESTIGATION

An issue focus enables both surfacing of the tacit components of culture (criterion 1) and comparisons across individuals and research settings (criterion 3). Given the ubiquitous nature of culture, organizational members cannot immediately reflect upon their cultural context and describe it verbally. Hence a key aspect in eliciting cognitive components is to provide a stimulus to respondents so that they are forced to make an interpretation based on their cognitive framework. The tacit aspects of culture will become apparent in the specific interpretations of respondents.

In addition comparisons can be made because the issue introduces a comparable context that forces interviewees to draw upon the same stock of knowledge. It channels attention to the same cultural aspects within a given cultural context. A comparison of these interpretations across respondents differentiates individually held opinions from *cultural beliefs*, defined as beliefs commonly held among the members of a group. The results of such a "group analysis" may identify subcultures that differ in their beliefs about the same issues (criterion 2).

For the selection of a specific issue, I established another three criteria. To qualify as an appropriate stimulus, the issue should

(1) be considered relevant by organizational members,
(2) be sensitive to culturally specific interpretations, and
(3) avoid systematic biases in data collection.

I will explain these criteria in turn.

Organizational Relevance and Meaning

Organizational members need to have accumulated knowledge about the issue under investigation so that they can talk about its various facets from their own perspective. We examined issues such as profit, growth, securing financial and natural resources, forecasting, competition, decision making, recruitment, selection, staffing, leadership, reward systems, control, corporate identity, social responsibility, productivity, technology, and innovation. All of these are necessary for an organization's operations and hence its survival. Not all of these are, however, of immediate relevance to employees at different hierarchic levels. Only a few people may be concerned with issues of corporate identity, corporate responsibility, profit, growth, competition, or market forecasts. Issues related to aspects of human resource management and work processes such as staffing, reward systems, benefits, leadership, technology, productivity, and innovation seem to have more meaning and direct relevance to a larger number of employees across an organization.

Sensitivity to Culturally Specific Interpretations

To reflect cultural cognitions, an issue must be defined in a customary rather than a factual way. A customary definition leaves latitude for culturally specific meanings and manifestations. Some issues in the above list fit this criteria better than others. Profit, for example, is likely to be defined in a factual way as financial gain or "the bottom line." Similar definitions and meanings of profit are likely to be found across organizations and industries without much cultural variation. The same is probably true for the issue of productivity. A well-developed technology is also likely to elicit rather standardized definitions and meanings, whereas technology specific to one company may not be revealed to an outsider if it is related to the organization's competitive advantage.

Leadership, staffing, reward systems, control, and innovation are issues that allow organizational variations and choices and that leave room for organization-specific expressions. Leadership may be defined and perceived as autocratic, paternalistic, democratic, supportive, or participatory. Knowledge about how it is enacted as well as suggestions for improvements and repair strategies are likely to differ according to the perceived leadership style in an organization or division. Questions about leadership may, however, be threatening to an employee, and he or she may withhold important information for fear of negative consequences. A third criterion was, therefore, established.

Avoiding Systematic Biases

The third criterion deals with the quality of data obtained. A high personal stake in an issue is likely to bias responses in a systematic way. Interviewees may withhold important information or give socially desirable answers, or their personal concerns may overshadow actual events. A researcher may not recognize these response biases and the "window dressing" of occurrences during short-term involvement.

Systematic response biases are more likely to occur with issues related to human resource management such as leadership, reward systems, and staffing than with innovation. The issue of innovation seemed to fit all established criteria well. I chose it, therefore, as stimulus to elicit culturally biased interpretations. I further specified innovation as "changes that made things different than before."

Innovation as a Projective Device

A review of the literature suggests that various authors consider some degree of innovation necessary for an organization's continued success whereas too much emphasis placed on innovation is considered undesirable if associated with high costs.[2] Furthermore the findings of a recent study on innovation in U.S. companies indicate that the issue of innovation "is closely linked with the 'world view' or 'culture' of organizations."[3] Sethia has developed this notion further in a paper in which he associates different managerial cultures with different degrees of organizational innovation.[4]

Opinions, definitions, and descriptions of innovation differ, how-ever, in scope and focus depending upon the authors' context and interests. This was an important characteristic of innovation in terms of this study because it gives latitude for culture-specific expressions and interpretations. Of interest to this study were those everyday conceptions about what is considered a major innovation within the company, accounts of how it came about, and who and what made it work in which context rather than theoretical (pre)conceptions or empirical findings about innovation.

To ensure that the answers were based on organizationally rele-vant knowledge, the researcher asked interviewees to describe at least three specific instances of the innovation that they considered most important within BIND. Comparisons of an individual's an-swers across the three instances indicated areas of consistencies and inconsistencies.

DESIGN OF SUCCESSIVE COMPARISONS

The nature of the research questions required an adaptive research design with an initial exploratory nature that would generate hypoth-eses that could then be investigated in a later phase. I chose the method of successive comparisons.[5] This design consists of several research phases moving from a first stage of inductive inquiry to the formulation and examination of hypotheses that are based on the results of the initial data gathering and analysis.

The lack of empirically based a priori knowledge and the topic under study required an investigation from the "inside" rather than from the "outside," in which categories and concepts are im-posed on respondents by the researcher.[6] Instead of imposing the categories and conceptions of the researcher as an outsider on re-spondents within the research site to gather data, the categories and conceptions should emerge from the research site.

This approach is similar to Glaser and Strauss's process of grounded theory research, in which patterned actions and interac-tions of individuals are discovered over time,[7] or that of ethno-graphic studies.[8] The approach used in this study differs, however, in its issue-specific focus, which makes it more pragmatic, less time-consuming, and hence more suitable to the field of management than to a general investigation of culture.

In this study the design consisted of five major phases to

(1) generate insider knowledge,
(2) extract themes from the data,
(3) further pursue these themes,
(4) probe the validity of an emerging hypothesis, and
(5) analyze and reanalyze all data collected.

The first phase was guided by a broad perspective. I conducted 10 interviews with top management and with people randomly selected from one of the firm's divisions (PC). The purpose of this data gathering and their analysis was to gain a basic understanding of the nature and functioning of the company and to ensure that the interviewing procedures were effective. This information also guided further decisions about the sampling of specific research sites within the company and the sampling of respondents. Whenever questions arose from the data during their analysis, I went back to the same respondents or other qualified organizational members and asked them the questions during the next visit to the research site.

During the second phase I predominantly focused on further data collection, their processing, and their preliminary analysis. Altogether 20 interviews were conducted during this phase with people randomly selected from the corporate headquarters (HQ) and from the PC division to further collect data and probe themes. Subsequently we analyzed the data from all 30 interviews conducted in phases one and two using thematic content analysis.[9] I describe this analysis in the section on data processing and data analysis below.

Ten interviews were conducted during phase three with people randomly selected from HQ and from PC. We used the interviews of this phase to further probe and validate the themes that had emerged from the initial content analysis in phase two. A hypothesis emerged from these data about cultural groupings. I pursued this hypothesis further in the last phase of data collection at another division of the same company.

To investigate the hypothesis that had emerged in phase three, I interviewed 12 individuals in phase four. They were selected randomly from a purposely chosen sample from BIND's third division.

After the data collection process was finished, I compiled all information gathered, reanalyzed it in detail, and interpreted it in the fifth stage. Even though all interview data were already "preanalyzed," a complete analysis of cultural themes could only be conducted after all data were in hand so that I could make multiple comparisons and contrasts. For reasons of objectivity all interview data were reanalyzed one month later. This procedures is described in the section on data processing below.

RESEARCH SITE

I selected a medium-sized, publicly held company with headquarters in Los Angeles as the research site. BIND was founded in 1952 as a "radio shop" selling electronic items. At the time of the study the company consisted of 29 divisions, predominantly located in the western part of the United States, with a total of 2,500 employees.[10]

BIND was divided into four major product groups: electronics, which accounted for 65% of sales and 72% of operating income; building products, accounting for 16% of sales and 15.3% of operating income; motor vehicle parts and accessories, with 8% of sales and 5.7% of operating income; and graphic arts, with 11% of the company's sales and 7% of operating income. Net sales were $312 million with $22 million in before-tax income and 11.25 million net income. With the exception of one manufacturing division in Northern California, which employed 500 people at the time of the study, 25 people work at the corporate office and approximately 90-100 in each division.

Based on company publications and initial interviews with the president of BIND and the vice president of finance, I decided to focus data collection on the corporate office and on one manufacturing division (PC) during the first two phases. In phase four of the study, I collected additional data in a Los Angeles-based graphic arts division (GA) of the company. Both divisions, PC and GA, had been acquired by BIND at about the same time, respectively, 16 and 19 years earlier. This time was considered sufficiently long for them to have adopted and integrated cultural aspects of BIND.

The manufacturing division was founded by BIND's current president in the early 1950s as a job shop that specialized in hydraulics. The job shop was acquired by BIND for a third of BIND's annual sales that year. The owner received stock and remained in his formerly owned company as general manager while his friend and partner moved to the corporate office. Within the year of PC's acquisition, 18 companies were acquired by BIND. BIND's stock plummeted. The general manager of the manufacturing division (PC)—the largest single shareholder—gathered with the other major individual shareholders and assumed presidency two years after the resignation of BIND's former president. The new president and five vice presidents formed an operations group. This group decided upon the corporation's basic structure, developed policies, and introduced management and control systems.

During the following decade of "housecleaning" and "pruning and cutting," the company was turned around.[11] From $50 million in sales and a $1 million loss in 1970, BIND advanced to $312 million in sales and $12 million in profit 14 years later.

At the time of the study PC was still a job shop. It specialized in the production of precision components used to produce airplanes and computer hardware. Components were produced to order according to designs submitted by customers. At that time the division employed over 100 people: a general manager; an administrative department with 4 people (a controller, one person responsible for accounting and personnel matters, two "office girls"); 3 sales people responsible for marketing and sales; 3 engineers; an inspection department with 1 inspection control manager and 4 inspectors; a plant manager and plant superintendent; 2 production control people (1 of whom was considered to be the general manager's assistant); 1 person handling shipping; a manager of the electronic subsystems, which was taken from an unprofitable division and moved to the PC division; a purchasing manager for the electronic subsystems; a quality control person; 45 welders and solderers of electronic circuit boards; and about 50 people working on the shop floor in five different departments (burring, rubber, grinding, drilling, and lathing). The president and two of the vice presidents had moved into the headquarters from this division.

For the last stage of data collection, I chose the GA division of BIND, which distributed film, chemicals, graphic arts supplies, and printing-related equipment such as large cameras and duplicating and copy machines. The division consisted of 82 people at the time of the research: 1 general manager, 1 sales manager responsible for equipment sales and another one responsible for supply sales, 1 administrative sales assistant, 28 sales people, 1 credit manager and his assistant, 1 division comptroller and 5 accountants, 1 office manager with 17 people at order and purchasing desks, 1 service manager with 5 people in the equipment service department, and 1 warehouse manager with 17 warehouse people.

Altogether I studied one company by collecting data from three different research sites. At the divisional level of analysis, these three sites can be considered three different divisions, including the corporate office, which was seen as a service division for the rest of the firm.

SAMPLE OF RESPONDENTS

I selected interviewees randomly from HQ and from different levels in PC during the first three phases of data collection. On a few occasions interviewees recommended a specific person for the next interview. This person was then contacted and interviewed. Because certain patterns emerged during the second phase of the research process, I used "theoretical sampling" as an additional sampling strategy. In phase four I selected interviewees to fit certain criteria to investigate the hypothesis that had emerged in phase three.

A total of 52 people were interviewed: 10 at HQ, 30 in PC, and 12 in GA. At HQ I conducted interviews with the president; 6 of the 7 vice presidents; the office manager, who was also the corporate comptroller and assistant to the vice president of finance; the internal audit manager; the corporate recruiter; and the major systems designer, who was in charge of developing and further refining BIND's computer system for its business operations.

The following people were interviewed at PC: the general manager, controller, accountant, both "office girls," all three salespeople, one engineer, the inspection manager and his four inspectors, the plant manager and superintendent, both production control people, the manager and purchasing manager of the electronic subsystems, three welders/solderers, and five shop-floor workers. Because most of the shop-floor workers were Spanish speaking, interviewing them was rather difficult and I decided not to conduct further interviews at this level.

At GA I conducted interviews with the general manager, both of the sales managers and the administrative sales assistant, three sales people, the office, warehouse, and credit managers, the comptroller, and the accountant.

METHODS OF DATA COLLECTION

Cognitive components are intangible and hence not directly observable. The most direct way to get to cognitions is through spoken language. Some recognized methods for the study of perceptions and cognitions are phenomenologically oriented interview techniques,[12] assumptional analysis,[13] or various forms of the Repertory Grid.[14] Existing interview techniques range from highly structured to completely unstructured with different degrees or involvement on the part of the interviewer. Massarik (1977) describes, for example, six different styles of interviews ranging from a complete disengagement of the interviewer in a highly structured approach—often practiced in market research—to a total involvement in the phenomenological interview.

The Interview Technique and Interview Process

In the context of this study I combined an issue-focused interview method with a phenomenological orientation, which focuses on the insiders' perspectives, their everyday theories of organizational life, and what they consider relevant in the given setting. It is highly flexible, and all of the issues brought up by the interviewee can be explored. During the interview the interviewer brackets his or her own assumptions about the issue under exploration so that his or her preconceptions do not influence the interviewee's answers.[15] Phenomenology involves a nonjudgmental orientation by suspending disbelief to allow the interviewee to unravel his or her story. That is, the researcher tries to avoid immediate value judgments about unfamiliar practices; to do so the researcher needs to make these value judgments explicit.[16] A purely phenomenological investigation is highly unstructured. The *issue focus* narrows and specifies the broad exploration. It provides an inherent structure for the interview process.

Assuming that organizational members hold a wide range of cultural knowledge, those components considered most important provide the best insights because they are most differentiated within a person's cognitive structure.[17] Each interviewee was, therefore, first asked to name those three innovations that he or she considered the most important.

After having named the three most important innovations, interviewees were asked to rank them, and the phenomenological exploration started usually with the most important one. To ensure that all relevant facets of an interviewee's organizational reality were explored, the researcher made sure that the following areas were covered at some point during the interview:

- Why is the mentioned innovation important?
- What was the context of the particular innovation?
- Who was involved and how?
- What made the innovation happen?
- What aspects or who presented obstacles in the process?
- What should or could have been done to improve it?
- What would you do differently now to make it better?

I also collected demographic information in the interview. I asked each respondent with whom he or she had to interact on a daily basis and with whom he or she liked to interact. I asked respondents about their educational and professional background both within and outside BIND, about their work experiences before joining the company, their positions held within the company, how they came to join BIND, and their professional goals for the future. These demographic data for the sample are listed in Table A.1.

I tape-recorded each interview and took notes. None of the respondents objected to the tape-recording, although the interviewer was asked on two occasions to discontinue recording for several minutes. In the very beginning of the interview, respondents were generally aware of the tape recorder. Their cautiousness disappeared, however, after several minutes.

At the beginning of each interview, I attempted first to establish some trust between myself and the interviewee and to make the respondent feel at ease. I considered my role as interviewer to be one of facilitating conditions conducive to the interviewee opening up and exploring the mentioned issues. This required a high degree of flexibility. Even if all the above questions were covered in each interview, their sequence may have been completely reversed. The objective was not to impose my ideas about culture upon the respondents but to help them explore and examine in detail the issues that they themselves had mentioned.

The emerging relationship between myself, as the interviewer, and the interviewee was used as a means to foster an in-depth exploration of surfacing phenomena. It could happen, for example, that a respondent would start questioning his or her initial—apparent—definition of innovation and reframe it in the course of the interview to adjust it to his or her experiential knowledge. Some respondents mentioned that a particular issue was never looked at in this way. It also happened that I listened to a respondent for some time without really understanding what the person was talking about. In the further course of the interview, pieces started to fall together and, after an

Table A.1 Demographics of Respondents

Variable	Total $n = 52$	Division 1 $n = 10$	Division 2 $n = 30$	Division 3 $n = 12$
Tenure (years):	10	11.35	8.53	10
Average Rank	0.1–23	1.5–17	0.1–23	1.25–21
Envisioned Career Steps:				
help make the company successful and grow	35	9	15	11
stay in the company and retire	11	1	9	1
leave the company for other type of work	3	1	9	1
no opinion yet (recently hired)	3	—	3	—
Entry:				
personal contact with somebody in the company	27	9	13	5
worked in other division/was acquired	8	—	4	4
was contacted by the company	5	1	3	1
through newspaper or sign at division	13	—	10	3
Education:				
professional training (C.P.A., M.B.A., engineer)	11	6	4	1
college degree	12	2	4	6
unfinished college education	5	2	2	1
high school	19	—	15	4
unfinished high school education	5	—	5	—
Training Within the Company:				
on-the-job training (people in skilled jobs are experienced and learn the specifics on the job; no formal training programs)	52	10	30	12

hour, I could understand the respondent's frame of reference from his or her point of view. The degree to which this was accomplished was tested by answering silently questions that I posed about issues being explored before the respondent gave his or her answers and explorations.

Interviews were scheduled to last one hour to allow enough time for such an exploration. They averaged about 50 minutes. If time pressures were initially present in the mind of the respondent, they seemed to disappear during the course of the interview. Posture, tone of voice, gestures, and flow in content revealed increasing involvement by respondents.

Observations

I made observations before, during, and after the interviews as well as on some specific occasions. During the interviews I observed the nonverbal behavior and compared it instantly with the verbal accounts. Other observations included the location and physical appearance of buildings, technical appliances, design and decoration of spaces, behaviors at the workplace, interactions, and transactions between people as well as their responses and behaviors toward the researcher as an outside person. I used these observations of behaviors and artifacts to validate or further explore information obtained in the interviews in a process of constant questioning, comparing, and contrasting. I asked organizational members about the specific meanings and context of certain behaviors and of observed artifacts such as certain machines, pictures, or "trophies."

Secondary Data

I also studied company publications such as the policy manual, the employee handbook, annual reports, and publications about the company. I compared and contrasted this information with findings from the other two information sources to determine its validity.

Altogether data were collected over a three-month period. Several entire days were spent at the manufacturing company and several half days in the graphic arts division.

DATA PROCESSING AND DATA ANALYSIS

Theoretical content analysis was used as the major technique for analyzing the data. Theoretical content analysis focuses on isolating and examining equivalent themes and their patterns rather than counting the occurrence of specific words as is practiced in classical content analysis.[18] I used a version of classical content analysis as an indicator for emphasis within the various accounts about innovations that were considered important.

Theoretical content analysis is a complex process composed of several interactive steps. In this study I needed to identify relevant statements about dictionary, directory, and recipe knowledge and understand their underlying meanings so that comparisons could be made across individuals. I had to identify converging as well as diverging themes before I could determine culturally relevant themes.

Condensing the Data

Each interview was tape-recorded and transcribed verbatim on the same or the following day. Information that seemed to suggest some pattern or theme was transferred to a separate document. This document was also used to record thoughts, reflections, and emerging ideas during the process of transcribing the interviews. If similar ideas or observations were expressed in subsequent interviews, they were marked and compared and contrasted with the earlier ones.

After all interviews had been conducted, transcribed, and pre-analyzed, I developed a format to organize the data in a more systematic way. This format was based on the structural components of cognitions and cultural knowledge as well as on the preliminary data analysis. *Descriptions of innovations* were isolated from the interviews and recorded as *dictionary information.* Accounts of *how they came about*—their context, place of occurrence, and people involved—were transcribed and kept as aspects of *directory information.* Statements about *improvements or repair strategies* were recorded as *recipe information.*

I listed *emphases and special concerns* of respondents separately as they constitute another important aspect of cultural knowledge.

Verbal expressions, tone of voice, and frequency in mentioning a certain aspect served as indicators of emphasis. Attitudes were recorded, including the object toward which the attitude was held; aspects that appeared to have the quality of a component or dimension of culture were listed in a separate area. In this way I condensed all interview transcripts, which averaged 25 pages, to relevant statements and organized them into a few pages.

After one month I repeated the process of identifying, condensing, and reorganizing all interview data to ensure objectivity. No significant changes were recorded between the first and the second analysis.

Theme Analysis

I then compiled all dictionary, directory, and recipe information a second time across all respondents to compare and contrast information about the same type of knowledge. Over a period of four weeks I extracted themes in various ways, applied them to the condensed interview-data format, and compared them with the data obtained from the observations. In addition a random sample of 12 full-length interviews was drawn from all interview transcripts. I reanalyzed each of them for themes in dictionary, directory, recipe knowledge, and emphases. The themes extracted in this analysis were then compared with the themes extracted from the entire list of dictionary, directory, and recipe knowledge. I related them to demographic information and compared them with categories and dimensions discussed by various authors in the managerial literature.

VALIDATING PROCEDURES, OBJECTIVITY, AND RELIABILITY

I used several procedures to ensure the validity, objectivity, and reliability of the data and their analysis.

Validating Procedures

To ensure the validity of verbal accounts, I compared them with the data collected from observations and documentary analysis. Verbal accounts may be only imperfect indicators of actual behavior. They can be biased in systematic as well as unsystematic ways. Respondents may want to be helpful and please the interviewer. They may conceal certain aspects or give accounts of desirable rather than actual conditions. Webb and coauthors[19] have, therefore, suggested a "triangulation" approach in data collection to minimize such problems of systematic biases. *Triangulation* refers to the study of the same phenomenon from different angles and different sources of information. It ensures internal validity of the data, which is otherwise difficult to obtain in qualitative research.

In processes of constantly comparing and contrasting[20] the data obtained from different sources, I identified converging themes and discrepancies. In the latter case I probed for more information to gain a better understanding of the nature of the discrepancies. Thus alternative explanations could also be stripped away.

In the next step I fed the identified themes back to selected interviewees to test their appropriateness. And the results of the study were presented to and discussed with top management. These discussions confirmed the accuracy and comprehensiveness of the obtained results.

Objectivity and Reliability

I was able to ensure objectivity and reliability in collecting, analyzing, and interpreting the results through three different procedures. During the interview I tested my understanding of the interviewee's perspective by posing questions. Before the interviewees answered, I answered the questions silently based on my understanding of the interviewees' perspective. The interview was continued until such an understanding was reached.

During the analysis and interpretation of the data, I discussed and debated the emerging themes critically with two colleagues who were informed about the research project without being actively involved in the research sites. Due to different training and cultural backgrounds, three different perspectives were used in a dialectical fashion to question the obtained data as well as their analysis.[21]

Furthermore no significant changes were noticed between the first data analysis and the second data analysis, which was conducted one month later. No changes needed to be made when the categories were reexamined during reanalysis.

EVALUATION OF THE METHODOLOGY

The developed methodology met the objectives. The focal method of data collection—the issue-focused interview with its phenomenological orientation—surfaced the tacit components of culture from the insiders' perspective. Its combination with the design of successive comparison made the methodology sensitive to surfacing different kinds of subcultures. And comparisons could be made across respondents and research sites.

More specifically the issue of innovation proved to be a useful projective device in getting to cultural knowledge because it made respondents reflect on concrete aspects of past behaviors within the company. The interview process revealed, however, that the term *innovation* is not equally well understood at different levels within the company. While it made people at middle and higher levels reflect about predominantly positive aspects of the company, the term was too abstract for employees at lower levels. At these levels it had to be specified in terms of changes that went on in the company, whereas at middle and higher levels this specification seemed to be unnecessary.

This finding has two implications for future research. It shows that the term *change* is more appropriate for use across hierarchic levels. The term *change* refers to habitual ways of thinking and behaving being revised and/or exchanged within an organization. The term helps, therefore, to surface those habits that are usually beyond reflection and that go unnoticed during daily activities.

In general this finding points to the issue that research instruments may have to be adjusted or translated if they are used to collect data across hierarchic levels. Only researchers conducting cross-cultural research have been aware of such necessities, but this finding demonstrates that translations may also be necessary in research involving a single company within one nation.

Furthermore the phenomenological orientation was unobtrusive in getting to cultural knowledge; it made the interview flexible and led to an open, holistic, and mutual exploration that yielded rich data. Each respondent's phenomenal world was unraveled rather than the interviewer's preconceptions about innovation or about cultural aspects of the company.

NOTES

1. This argument is supported by several authors such as Kaplan (1964), Van Maanen (1979), Evered and Louis (1981), Crozier and Friedberg (1983), and Fetterman (1989).

2. See, for example, Burns (1975), Goodman and Abernathy (1978), and Minard (1983).

3. This study was conducted by O'Toole (1982).

4. Sethia (1983).

5. Turner (1967) and Diesing (1971) developed and applied this method.

6. The differences between an "inquiry from the inside" and an "inquiry from the outside" are discussed in Evered and Louis (1981) or Fetterman (1989).

7. Glaser and Strauss (1967)

8. See, for example, Leiter (1980), Spradley (1980), or Fetterman (1989).

9. Carney (1972) discusses the different kinds of content analysis.

10. All numbers refer to the year in which I conducted the study.

11. The two metaphors "housecleaning" and "pruning and cutting" were used by the company's president to describe his activity during the first 12 years in his presidential role.

12. See, for example, Massarik (1977).

13. See, for example, Mason and Mitroff (1981) or Mitroff et al. (1979).

14. See, for example, Bannister (1977), Kelly (1955), or Wacker (1979).

15. The reader who is interested in phenomenology is referred to Heidegger (1977), Husserl (1975), Leiter (1980), or Massarik (1977).

16. Kaplan (1964), Denzin (1989), or Fetterman (1989) discuss the influence of values in research and procedures and how to avoid their unreflected influence.

17. This is further explored by Schroder, Driver, and Streufert (1967).

18. Carney (1979) gives a detailed description of theoretical content analysis.

19. Webb, Campbell, Schwartz, and Sechrest (1966).

20. Glaser and Strauss (1967) describe such an approach for developing grounded theory.

21. The three perspectives were strategic, technological, and behavioral with U.S., U.S.-Jamaican, and European backgrounds.

APPENDIX B

Some Questions for Future Research

The following questions give some specific directions for future research in the area of cultural dynamics in organizational settings.

Question 1. If incentive and reward structures are consistent with the functions within a division of a company, do cultural groupings form according to perceived functional domains in regards to the dictionary knowledge?

Question 2. Are cultural groupings that form according to functional domains in regard to dictionary knowledge and that complement each other a prerequisite for organizational effectiveness?

Question 3. Are cultural groupings in regard to dictionary knowledge that form according to noncomplementary functional domains indicative of ineffectiveness of a division or company?

Question 4. Are cultural groupings that do not form according to functional domains in regard to dictionary knowledge associated with performance problems?

Question 5. Are inconsistencies between incentive/reward systems and perceived functional domains in regard to dictionary knowledge associated with cultural groupings that reflect internal politics?

Question 6. If cultural groupings form according to functional domains in regard to dictionary knowledge across divisions, is the interpretation of these functional domains at the divisional level influenced by the division's identity? (*Identity* is defined in terms of its major products, skills, and technology.)

Question 7. To what extent do the emphases of equivalent cultural groupings (in regard to dictionary knowledge) differ in divisions with similar divisional identities as compared to divisions with differing divisional identities? (Equivalent groupings are, for example, two marketing groupings if they form according to functional domains in terms of the dictionary type of cultural knowledge.)

Question 8. To what extent does the degree of centralization within a firm influence the degree of congruence between equivalent functional groupings in divisions with similar identities?

Question 9. To what extent is the degree of centralization associated with the degree of congruence in dictionary, directory, and recipe knowledge between equivalent functional groupings of divisions with similar identities?

Question 10. To what extent are functional domain groupings in regard to directory knowledge associated with problems of internal integration and coordination?

Question 11. To what extent is the formation of cultural groupings other than according to functional domains with regard to dictionary knowledge associated with low performance and a high degree of internal politics?

Question 12. To what extent is the amount of recipe knowledge that supports directory knowledge associated with the degree of internal politics?

Question 13. To what extent is a large amount of recipe knowledge that differs from the directory knowledge associated with dissatisfaction, a high degree of internal politics, and low performance?

Question 14. To what extent does the cultural knowledge map capture cultural knowledge in other organizations and help in gaining an understanding of these cultural settings?

These questions are not conclusive. They represent a sample of specific possibilities that may be of interest to researchers for further investigation.

APPENDIX C

Epilogue

The phenomenon "organizational culture" had caught my interest a long time ago. During my doctoral studies at UCLA, I took a course in organizational development with Tony Raia, and my self-selected term project explored possibilities of diagnosing organizational culture. Several recognized authors in the field of organizational development for whom I have a great deal of respect—including Warren Bennis, Warner Burke, and Edgar Schein—emphasized the importance of culture in change processes. This emphasis showed in sentences such as this one: "If you want to change an organization you have to change its culture." But what is it, this culture? A few paragraphs devoted to culture in voluminous books appeared as traces rather than revelations about the phenomenon, and they caused me to question the importance of the concept.

My search for diagnostic possibilities began with questionnaires—none of which seemed to get to the essence of the phenomenon—and ended with a quote from Warner Burke, who stated that nothing could replace his "personal antenna" in diagnosing culture. His words made sense but I wanted something more tangible, less subjective. Then Noel Tichy's findings about practicing organizational diagnosticians made me wonder about *what* I was looking for in my diagnostic search. What were people's conceptions of the phenomenon that framed and biased their perceptions in looking for and writing about organizational culture?

I could not solve the problem that quarter; I handed in my paper still dissatisfied with what I had reported. My personal experiences in different organizations, in different countries, and in equivalent institutions located in different countries told me that there were more relevant things to report. Whenever I had made a transition, I saw the differences more clearly—differences between people's way of thinking, behaving, interrelating, and dressing; their expectations about a certain type of work and, for example, their conceptions of good research. After a while the differences started to blur, my visitor's or tourist perspective disappeared, and I was slowly enveloped in the "normality" of those people and the things that were around me day after day.

My interest in culture was subsequently sparked in a small seminar on issues in organizational theory with Rodolfo Alvarez. I used this setting to explore the concept of culture in organizational contexts in more depth and from a different angle than I had before. Our discussions were provoking and stimulating, and my paper, which presented a framework for studying organizational culture, was based on pure theoretical speculations because there were hardly any publications on the topic at the time. I had no idea how quickly this would change: Within the period of a year, books and articles with *culture* in their title were everywhere, it seemed. I was thrilled and disappointed at the same time. On the one hand it meant that, after all, the phenomenon of culture seemed to be of recognized—rather than implied—importance to organizations. On the other hand it meant that others had explored *my* topic. However, the so-called state-of-the-art literature did not reveal very much of the phenomenon.

One day I ran into Maggi Phillips, at the time a doctoral student at UCLA's Graduate School of Management, who was interested in the same topic. She asked me what I thought about the idea of meeting regularly to bounce around some ideas. And Richard Goodman—a professor in her area of concentration—might be interested in joining our meetings as he had developed an interest in the topic from a different perspective. This was the initiation of our weekly "culture club" meetings. As we discovered later, each of us had intensive and extensive firsthand experiences of living in different cultures, which had no doubt evoked our interest in the subject.

The discussions with Dick Goodman and Maggi Phillips were encouraging, inspiring, energizing, and comforting. They allowed an exploration of theoretical issues without immediate judgments; they gave me enough support and reinforcement to stick to my elusive subject.

Later, when I brought back my data and stories from the research sites, the two listened to them and discussed them with curiosity, vehemence, and, at times, with astonishing doubt because they seemed to refute some of the ideas we had discussed earlier in the year. At least we had some real data from "the real world out there" to deal with rather than somebody else's opinion.

When I began to contact companies, I started out with a list of about 25, which was soon reduced to 12. Three firms expressed their disinterest; four were interested but felt they could not afford the required time at the moment. "Can you call back in, say, four or six months?" was a common reply. Seven companies asked for a written proposal, and three of these expressed their conditional interest, based on first overcoming internal turbulence. In three of the remaining companies, some individuals were highly supportive of the proposed study while others seemed to be opposed. The proponents saw the potential benefits of such a study while the opponents feared revealing sensitive areas. Decisions were prolonged over several weeks, which caused me to question the feasibility of using any of these companies as a research site. Some of my phone calls were quite frustrating: being put on hold for several minutes, not being able to pin down the person in charge, and not having calls returned.

Things were quite different in the company that I finally chose as my research site. I had a phone number taken from a directory that also briefly described the company. I dialed the number and had the president on the line. Because I had expected first to make my way through several layers of secretaries, I had to take a deep breath before I explained my project to him. He listened and promptly replied that he was interested in participating in my study. However, if I wanted to interview him, I had to come the next day because he was leaving for a two-week trip the following day. I was startled. I had expected to find a company soon, but this fast entry was almost too good to be true.

The next day I went to interview the president, a sincere, direct, reflective, personable, and—using Carl Rogers's term—"authentic" person. I was astonished by the language and metaphors he used—no vocabulary that belonged to the military. Instead he used psychologically oriented terms and metaphors from gardening and housekeeping. He left it up to me to decide where I wanted to focus my study of the company, which division I wanted to use, and whom I wanted to interview. He tried to give me as much information as possible so that I could make my decisions. He referred me to his "associate," a vice president whom I could contact next who could also help me in case of any questions or problems that I might encounter during his absence. The vice president would also provide me with a letter I had requested authorizing me to talk with people in the divisions.

As it turned out I did not need such a letter. My initial interaction with the president—beginning with my phone call and the interview, which ended long after office hours as we took the elevator to the lobby—turned out to be the rule rather than the exception in my encounters at BIND. None of my scheduled interviews was canceled and none of them started more than five minutes later than scheduled. When I had contacted someone for an interview, I received a prompt appointment. People took time to talk to me; they were sincere, open, and helpful. They gave me quite a bit of their time and showed me around when I expressed interest in certain aspects of their work.

I was surprised by the pace of the work. I have rarely seen such a busy place: People were constantly working, running around, interacting with each other, sitting over paperwork, or answering the phone. I never had the feeling that they did this for show or that somebody pressed them to work so hard—except on the shop floor of the PC division. But, even there, people were autonomous in changing workstations or working at their own pace, which is rewarded accordingly.

I was struck by the humanistic orientation within the company personified by the president—a humanism à la Américaine: It is up to the person where he or she will go within the company. BIND is one of the most people-oriented companies I can remember having encountered as an insider or outsider—at least in the United States. With the president as a consistent, sincere, and congruent role model, top management expressed genuine concern about the well-being of their employees that could be considered beyond their obligations. Unanimously they agreed—implicitly or explicitly—that the most difficult decision they ever had to make was to fire a person, but they were aware of the fact that they had first tried everything possible to avoid the situation.

This concern about their employees seemed to be ingrained in whatever they said or did—a way of life reciprocated by lower-level employees. The president's annual trophies for outstanding

divisional performances given to the general managers were reciprocated with a metal picture of BIND's business locations given to top
management by the general managers. The dedication of the general
manager in the GA division to developing the sales force was reciprocated by an engraved "Thank You" from the sales people that he
described as "a very touching thing."

Surprising also was the care given to details. Top management's
beliefs in frequent interactions, in direct communications, and in
no-frills management was even reflected in their office layout. The
four "office girls" were located in a central room with the offices of
the president and vice presidents located around this room. One of
the vice presidents was specially designated to design and redesign
new and existing facilities based on years of accumulated experience.

After I had finished several interviews, I began to dislike my
method. I realized its power in surfacing the information I wanted,
but so many avenues were opened in the course of the interview that
it required a great deal of discipline to cover those issues that I needed
for comparisons. I started to feel stupid—having to explore the same
issues over and over again even if I knew the answers. For reasons of
reliability I had to force myself to do it. The next time I will probably
use at least two interviewers trained in the method to avoid the
personal feeling of redundancy.

I am also aware to what extent the context of my study biased my
results. On the one hand I wanted this bias because it reveals the
peculiar cultural aspects of that company. On the other hand I realize
that the study is lacking in data. The nature of the company does not
leave much room for politics, and top management felt in a strong
position to show their accomplishments to an outsider. Had I been
allowed entry into a troubled company, my quotes from the interviews might have been full of negative instead of positive examples.
And the process "task accomplishment" might have been characterized by "cover your back" and "get aligned with the people in power"
rather than by autonomy and team effort. Access to troubled organizations is, unfortunately, difficult if not impossible in the role of a
researcher while access to them by consultants is readily accepted.
Closer links between research and consulting or research-oriented
consulting may, therefore, be increasingly necessary in the future
because historical—after-the-fact—analyses are difficult and based on
highly selective information.

Overall I must say that I enjoyed the data collection process tremen-
dously. I learned quite a bit—about the people I interviewed, about

aspects of the company as well about the usefulness of the theoretical models within the field of organizational and behavioral science that I had assimilated over the years. What I realized quickly was that "culture" is a much more elusive concept than I even dared dream when I started out in the area, that it is much more closely related to the philosophy and personal beliefs of the leader—at least at BIND—than I had initially thought.

At this point many questions have emerged from my study that need further investigation. But, having experienced firsthand the power of cultural knowledge in organizations, I think it will be exciting to further explore this phenomenon.

References

Adelung, J. C. (1773). Grammatikalisch-kritisches Wörterbuch der hoch-deutschen Mundart [Grammatically critical dictionary of high German language]. In *Zweyte vermehrte und verbesserte Ausgabe* (pp. 1354-1355). Leipzig, Germany: Erster Theil.

Allen, R. F. (1984, October 24-27). *A systematic norm based methodology for bringing about change.* Paper presented at the conference "Managing Corporate Cultures," Pittsburgh.

Ansoff, H. I. (1979). *Strategic management.* New York: John Wiley.

Baker, E. L. (1980, July). Managing organizational culture. *Management Review,* pp. 8-13.

Bannister, D. (Ed.). (1977). *New perspectives in personal construct theory.* London: Academic Press.

Barney, J. B. (1986). Organizational culture: Can it be a sustained source of competitive advantage? *Academy of Management Review, 11*(3), 656-665.

Benedict, R. (1934). *Patterns of culture.* New York: Houghton Mifflin.

Benedict, R. (1942). Anthropology and culture change. *American Scholar, 11,* 243-248.

Berg, P. (1983, March). *Symbolic management of organizational cultures.* Paper presented at the "Organizational Folklore Conference, Santa Monica, CA.

Berger, P. L., & Luckmann, T. (1966). *The social construction of reality.* New York: Penguin.

Boas, F. (1896). The limitations of the comparative method of anthropology. In F. Boas, *Race, language and culture* (Reprint; pp. 271-304). New York: Macmillan.

Boas, F. (1940). *Race, language and culture.* New York: Macmillan.

Brown, M. A. (1976, October). Values: A necessary but neglected ingredient of motivation on the job. *Academy of Management Review,* pp. 15-23.

Burns, R. O. L. (1975). *Innovation: The management connection.* London: Heath.

206

Cameron, K. S. (1984, June). *Cultural congruence, strength and type: Relationships to effectiveness.* Unpublished manuscript, National Center for Higher Educational Management Systems, Boulder, CO.

Campbell, B. (1966). *Human evolution.* Chicago: Aldine.

Campbell, D., & Stanley, J. (1974). *Experimental and quasi-experimental design for research.* Chicago: Rand McNally.

Carney, T. F. (1979). *Content analysis: A technique for systematic inference from communications.* Winnipeg, Canada: University of Manitoba Press.

Chandler, A. (1962). *Strategy and structure: Chapters in the history of American industrial enterprise.* Cambridge: MIT Press.

Chase, S. (1948). *The proper study of mankind.* New York: Harper & Row.

Corporate culture: The hard-to-change values that spell success or failure. (1980, October 27). *Business Week,* pp. 148-159.

Crozier, M., & Friedberg, E. (1983). *Actions and systems: The politics of collective action.* Chicago: University of Chicago Press.

Davis, S. (1984). *Managing corporate cultures.* Cambridge, MA: Ballinger.

Deal, T., & Kennedy, A. (1982). *Corporate cultures.* Reading, MA: Addison-Wesley.

Denison, D. R. (1984, Winter). Bringing corporate culture to the bottom line. *Organizational Dynamics,* pp. 5-22.

Denzin, N. K. (1989). *Interpretive interactionism* (Applied Social Research Methods Series, No. 16). Newbury Park, CA: Sage.

Diesing, P. (1971). *Patterns of discovery in the sciences.* Chicago: Aldine-Atherton.

Donaldson, G., & Lorsch, J. (1983). *Decision making at the top: The shaping of strategic direction.* New York: Basic Books.

Dutton, J. E., & Duncan, R. B. (1987a). The influence of the strategic planning process on strategic change. *Strategic Management Journal, 8*(2), 103-116.

Dutton, J. E., & Duncan, R. B. (1987b). The creation of momentum for change through the process of strategic issue diagnosis. *Strategic Management Journal, 8*(3), 279-295.

Evered, R., & Louis, M. R. (1981). Alternative perspectives in the organizational sciences: "Inquiries from the inside" and "inquiries from the outside." *Academy of Management Review, 6*(3), 385-389.

Fetterman, D. M. (1989). *Ethnography step by step* (Applied Social Research Methods Series, No. 17). Newbury Park, CA: Sage.

Foa, U. G., & Foa, E. B. (1974). *Societal studies of mind.* Springfield, IL: Charles C Thomas.

Freeman, D. (1970). Human nature and culture. In *Man and the new biology* (pp. 50-75). Canberra: Australian National University Press.

Gans, H. J. (1967). *The Leavittowners.* New York: Pantheon.

Garfinkel, H. (1967). *Studies in ethnomethodology.* Englewood Cliffs, NJ: Prentice-Hall.

Geertz, C. (1973). *The interpretation of cultures.* New York: Basic Books.

Glaser, B. G., & Strauss, A. L. (1967). *The discovery of grounded theory: Strategies for qualitative research.* Chicago: Aldine.

Goodenough, W. H. (1971). *Culture, language and society.* Reading, MA: Addison-Wesley.

Goodman, R. A., & Abernathy, W. J. (1978). The contribution of "new boy" phenomena to increasing innovation and development in new technology. *R & D Management, 9*(1), 33-41.

Gregory, K. L. (1983). Native-view paradigms: Multiple cultures and culture conflicts in organizations. *Administrative Science Quarterly, 28*(3), 359-376.

Greiner, L. (1979). Patterns of organizational change. *Harvard Business Review, 45*(3), 119-130.

Grinyer, P. H., & Spender, J. (1979). Recipes, crises and adaptation in mature business. *International Studies of Management and Organization, 9*(3), 113-133.

Gupta, A. K., & Stengrevics, J. M. (1983, August). *Strategy, culture and climate: A conceptual re-evaluation* (Working paper No. 32/83). Boston: Boston University, School of Management.

Handy, C. B. (1978). Zur Entwicklung der Organisationskultur durch Management Development Methoden [Developing organizational culture through management development]. *Zeitschrift für Organisation, 7*, 404-410.

Harris, M. (1964). *The nature of cultural things.* New York: Random House.

Harris, M. (1968). *The rise of anthropological theory.* New York: Thomas Y. Crowell.

Harrison, R. (1972, May/June). Understanding your organizational character. *Harvard Business Review*, pp. 119-128.

Hatch, E. (1973). *Theories of man and culture.* New York: Columbia University Press.

Hedberg, B., & Jönsson, S. (1977). Strategy formulation as a discontinuous process. *International Studies of Management & Organization, 7*, 88-109.

Heidegger, M. (1977). *Basic writings.* New York: Harper & Row.

Herder, J. G. (1784). *Ideen zur Philosophie der Geschichte der Menschheit* [Ideas on the philosophy of the history of mankind]. Leipzig, Germany: Erster Theil.

Herskovits, M. J. (1924). A preliminary consideration of the culture areas of Africa. *American Anthropologist, 26*, 50-63.

Herzberg, F. (1966). *Work and the nature of man.* Cleveland: World.

Herzberg, F., Mausner, B., & Snyderman, B. (1959). *The motivation to work.* New York: Wiley.

Hofstede, G. (1980). *Culture's consequences: International differences in work-related values.* Beverly Hills, CA: Sage.

Homans, G. G. (1950). *The human group.* New York: Harcourt, Brace & World.

Husserl, E. (1948). Phenomenology. In *Encyclopaedia Britannica* (Vol. 17, pp. 699-702, 14th ed.). Chicago: Encyclopaedia Britannica. (Original work published 1928)

Husserl, E. (1975). *Ideas: General introduction to pure phenomenology.* New York: Collier.

Janis, I. L. (1972). *Victims of groupthink.* Boston: Houghton Mifflin.

Justis, R. T., Judd, R. J., & Stephens, D. B. (1985). *Strategic management and policy.* Englewood Cliffs, NJ: Prentice-Hall.

Kaplan, A. (1964). *The conduct of inquiry.* Scranton, PA: Chandler.

Keesing, R. M. (1974). Theories of culture. *Annual Review of Anthropology, 3*, 73-97.

Keesing, R. M. (1976). *Cultural anthropology: A contemporary perspective.* New York: Holt, Rinehart & Winston.

Keesing, R. M., & Keesing, F. M. (1971). *New perspectives in cultural anthropology.* New York: Holt, Rinehart & Winston.

Kelly, G. A. (1955). *The psychology of personal construct theory: Vol. 1. A theory of personality.* New York: Norton.

Kelly, H. H. (1979). *Personal relationships: Their structures and processes.* New York: Halstead.

Kilmann, R. H., & Saxton, M. J. (1983). *Kilmann-Saxton Culture-Gap survey.* Pittsburgh: Organization Design Consultants.

Kimberly, J. R., & Miles, R. H. (1980). *Organizational life cycles.* San Francisco: Jossey-Bass.

Kluckhohn, C. K. (1951). The study of culture. In D. Lerner & H. D. L. Losswell (Eds.), *The political sciences.* Stanford, CA: Stanford University Press.

Kluckhohn, F. R., & Strodbeck, F. L. (1961). *Variations in value orientations.* New York: Row, Peterson.

Knigge, A. F. (1977). Über den Umgang mit Menschen [Dealing with people] (Gert Ueding, Ed.). Frankfurt am Main: Insel. (1st and 2nd eds., 1788; revised 1790)

Kobi, J. M., & Wüthrich, H. A. (1986). *Unternehmenskultur verstehen, erfassen und gestalten* [Understanding, assessing and managing corporate culture]. Landsberg/Lech: Verglag Moderne Industrie.

Kroeber, A. L. (1917). The superorganic. *American Anthropologist, 19,* 163-213.

Kroeber, A. L., & Kluckhohn, C. K. (1952). *Culture: A critical review of concepts and definitions* (Peabody Museum of Archeology and Ethnology Papers, No. 47). Cambridge, MA: Harvard University.

Kruse, L. M. (1975). Teenage drinking and sociability. *Urban Life and Culture, 4,* 54-78.

Langness, L. L. (1979). *The study of culture.* San Francisco: Chandler & Sharp.

Leiter, K. (1980). *A primer on ethnomethodology.* New York: Oxford University Press.

Lenz, R. T. (1985). Paralysis by analysis: Is your planning system becoming too rational. *LRP, 18*(4), 64-72.

LeVine, R. A. (1954). *Culture, behavior and personality.* Chicago: Aldine.

Lévi-Strauss, C. (1949). *Les structures élémentaires de la parenté.* Paris: Presses Universitaires de France. (English translation, 1969, The elementary structures of kinship. Boston: Beacon.)

Likert, R. (1967). *The human organization.* New York: McGraw-Hill.

Lipp, W. (1979). Kulturtypen, kulturelle Symbole, Handlungswelt: Zur Plurivalenz von Kultur [Culture types, cultural symbols, world of action: The pluralism of culture]. *Kölner Zeitschrift für Soziologie und Sozialpsychologie, 31,* 450-484.

Lorsch, J. W. (1985). Strategic myopia: Culture as an invisible barrier to change. In R. H. Kilmann, M. J. Saxton, & R. Serpa (Eds.), *Gaining control of the corporate culture* (pp. 84-102). San Francisco: Jossey-Bass.

Lorsch, J. W., & Lawrence, P. R. (1965). Organizing for product innovation. *Harvard Business Review, 43*(1), 109-122.

Lubbock, J. (1912). *The origin of civilization and the primitive condition of man.* London: Longman, Green. (Original work published 1879)

Luckmann, T. (1981). Einige Überlegungen zu Alltagswissen und Wissenschaft [Some thoughts about everyday knowledge and science]. *Pädagogische Rundschau, 35*(1), 91-109.

Mahdi, (1971). *Ibn Khaldun's philosophy of history.* Chicago: University of Chicago Press.

Mair, L. (1934). *An African people in the twentieth century.* London: Routledge.

Malinowski, B. (1939). Review of six essays on culture by Albert Blumenthal. *American Sociological Review, 4*, 588-592.

Malinowski, B. (1944). *A scientific theory of culture.* Chapel Hill: University of North Carolina Press.

Martin, J. (1982). Stories and scripts in organizational settings. In A. Hastorf & A. Isen (Eds.), *Cognitive social psychology* (pp. 255-305). New York: Elsevier.

Martin, J., Sitkin, S., & Boehm, M. (1983). *Wild-eyed guys and old salts: The emergence and disappearance of organizational subcultures* (Working paper). Stanford, CA: Stanford University, Graduate School of Business.

Mason, R. O. (1969). A dialectical approach to strategic planning. *Management Science, 15*(8), 403-414.

Mason, R. O., & Mitroff, I. I. (1981). *Challenging strategic planning assumptions.* New York: John Wiley.

Massarik, F. (1977). *The science of perceiving: Foundations for an empirical phenomenology* (Working paper). Los Angeles: University of California, Graduate School of Management.

Mead, M. (1939). *From the South Seas.* New York: Morrow.

Meggit, M. (1965). *The lineage system of the Mea Enga of New Guinea.* Edinburgh: Oliver and Boyd.

Miller, D., & Mintzberg, H. (1974). *Strategy formulation in context: Some tentative models* (Working paper). Montreal, Canada: McGill University.

Minard, L. (1983, July 4). Can Europe catch up? *Forbes,* pp. 84-92.

Mitroff, I. (1983). *Stakeholders of the organizational mind.* San Francisco: Jossey-Bass.

Mitroff, I. I., Emshoff, J. F., & Kilmann, R. H. (1979). Assumptional analysis: A methodology for strategic problem solving. *Management Science, 25*(6), 583-593.

O'Toole J. (1982). *Declining innovation: The failure of success* (Summary Report of the Seventh Twenty Year Forecast Project). Los Angeles: University of Southern California, Center for Futures Research.

Parsons, T., & Shils, E. A. (1951). *Toward a general theory of action.* Cambridge, MA: Harvard University Press.

Pascale, R. T., & Athos, A. G. (1981). *The art of Japanese management.* New York: Simon & Schuster.

Peters, T. J. (1978, Autumn). Symbols, patterns, and settings: An optimistic case for getting things done. *Organizational Dynamics,* pp. 3-23.

Peters, T. J. (1984, October 24-27). *In search of excellence: Lessons from America's best-run companies.* Presentation given at the conference "Managing Corporate Cultures," Pittsburgh.

Peters, T. J., & Waterman, R. H. (1982). *In search of excellence: Lessons from America's best-run companies.* New York: Harper & Row.

Pettigrew, A. M. (1979). On studying organizational cultures. *Administrative Science Quarterly, 24*, 570-581.

Phillips, M. E. (1984). *A conception of culture in organizational settings* (Working paper No. 8-84). Los Angeles: University of California, Graduate School of Management.

Phillips, M. E. (1990). *Industry as a cultural grouping.* Unpublished doctoral dissertation, University of California, Los Angeles.

Pike, K. (1954). *Language in relation to a unified theory of the structure of human behavior* (Vol. 1). Glendale, CA: Summer Institute of Linguistics.

Porter, M. E. (1980). *Competitive strategy.* New York: Free Press.

Preszeworski, A., & Teune, H. (1970). *The logic of comparative social inquiry.* New York: John Wiley.

Pümpin, C. (1984, May 3). *Unternehmenskultur, Unternehmensstrategie und Unternehmenserfolg* [Corporate culture, corporate strategy and corporate performance]. Paper presented at the ATAG Conference "Die Bedeutung der Unternehmenskultur für den künftigen Erfolg Ihres Unternehmens" [The importance of corporate culture for the future success of your firm], Zurich.

Radcliffe-Brown, A. R. (1922). *The Andaman islanders.* Glencoe, IL: Free Press.

Radcliffe-Brown, A. R. (1952). *Structure and function in primitive society.* London: Dohen and West.

Radcliffe-Brown, A. R. (1957). *A natural science of society.* Glencoe, IL: Free Press.

Rogers, C. (1961). *On becoming a person.* Boston: Houghton-Mifflin.

Rokeach, M. (1975). *The nature of human values.* New York: Free Press.

Rosnow, R. L., & Fine, G. A. (1976). *Humor and gossip: The social psychology of hearsay.* New York: Elsevier.

Sackmann, S. A. (1983). Organisationskultur: die unsichtbare Einflussgrösse [Organizational culture: The invisible influence]. *Gruppendynamik, 4,* 393-406.

Sackmann, S. A. (1990). Managing organizational culture: Dreams and possibilities. In J. A. Anderson (Ed.), *Communication yearbook* (Vol. 13). Newbury Park, CA: Sage.

Sapienza, A. M. (1985). Believing is seeing: How organizational culture influences the decisions top managers make. In R. H. Kilmann, M. J. Saxton, & R. Serpa (Eds.), *Gaining control of the corporate culture* (pp. 66-83). San Francisco: Jossey-Bass.

Sapir, E. (1917). Do we need a superorganic? *American Anthropologist, 19,* 441-447.

Sathe, V. (1983, Autumn). Some action implications of corporate culture. *Organizational Dynamics,* pp. 5-23.

Schank, R. C., & Abelson, R. P. (1977). *Scripts, plans, goals, and understanding.* Hillsdale, NJ: Lawrence Erlbaum.

Schein, E. H. (1983, Summer). The role of the founder in creating organizational culture. *Organizational Dynamics,* pp. 13-28.

Schein, E. H. (1984, Winter). Coming to a new awareness of organizational culture. *Sloan Management Review,* pp. 3-16.

Schein, E. H. (1985). *Organizational culture and leadership: A dynamic view.* San Francisco: Jossey-Bass.

Schroder, H. M., Driver, M. J., & Streufert, S. (1967). *Human information processing: Individuals and groups functioning in complex social situations.* New York: Holt, Rinehart & Winston.

Schütz, A. (1945). Some leading concepts of phenomenology. *Social Research, 12*, 77-97.

Schütz, A. (1962). *Collected papers: Vol. 1. The problem of reality* (M. Natanson, Ed.). The Hague, the Netherlands: Martinus Nijhoff.

Schwartz, H., & Davis, S. (1981). Matching corporate culture and business strategy. *Organizational Dynamics, 10*(1), 30-48.

Scott, W. R. (1981). *Organizations: Rational, natural, and open systems.* Englewood Cliffs, NJ: Prentice-Hall.

Selltiz, C., Wrightsman, C., & Cook, S. (1981). *Research methods in social relations* (4th ed.). New York: Holt, Rinehart & Winston.

Selznick, P. (1957). *Leadership in administration: A sociological interpretation.* New York: Row, Peterson.

Sethia, N. (1983). *Implications of organizational culture for innovation.* Unpublished manuscript, National Institute of Banking Management, Bombay.

Sherif, C. W., Sherif, M., & Nebergall, R. E. (1965). *Attitude and attitude change: The social judgement-involvement approach.* Philadelphia: W. B. Saunders.

Shibutani, T. (1962). Reference groups and social control. In A. M. Rose (Ed.), *Human behavior and social processes: An interactionist approach.* Boston: Houghton Mifflin.

Silverman, D. (1971). *The theory of organizations: A sociological framework.* New York: Basic Books.

Silverzweig, S., & Allen, R. F. (1976). Changing the corporate culture. *Sloan Management Review, 17*(3), 33-50.

Smircich, L. (1983). Concepts of culture and organizational analysis. *Administrative Science Quarterly, 28*, 339-358.

Spradley, J. P. (1972). *Culture and cognition: Rules, maps and plans.* New York: Chandler.

Spradley, J. P. (1980). *Participant observation.* New York: Holt, Rinehart & Winston.

Spradley, J. P., & Mann, B. (1975). *The cocktail waitress: Women's work in a male world.* New York: John Wiley.

Steward, J. (1955). *Theory of culture change.* Urbana: University of Illinois Press.

Sussman, L., Ricchio, P., & Behohlav, J. (1983). Corporate speeches as a source of corporate values: An analysis across years, themes and industries. *Strategic Management Journal, 1-2*, 187-196.

Taylor, S. E., & Fiske, S. T. (1981). Getting inside the head: Methodologies for process analysis in attribution and social cognition. In J. H. Harvey, W. Ickes, & R. F. Kidd (Eds.), *New directions in attribution research* (Vol. 3). Hillsdale, NJ: Lawrence Erlbaum.

Tichy, M. (1975). How different types of change agents diagnose organizations. *Human Relations, 28*(9), 771-779.

Tolman, E. C. (1948). Cognitive maps in rats and man. *Psychological Review, 5*, 189-202.

Trice, H. M., Belasco, J. E., & Allutto, J. A. (1969). The role of ceremonies in organization behavior. *Industrial and Labor Relations Review, 23*(1), 40-51.

Tunstall, W. B. (1983, Fall). Cultural transition at At&T. *Sloan Management Review*, pp. 15-26.

Turner, V. (1967). *The forest of symbols.* Ithaca, NY: Cornell University Press.

Tylor, E. B. (1971). *Primitive culture: Researches into the development of mythology, philosophy, religion, language, art and custom.* London: J. Murray, 2 vols. (1903).

Van de Ven, A. H. (1983). *Creating and sustaining a corporate culture in fast changing organizations.* Presentation at the Executive Seminar on Corporate Excellence, University of Santa Clara, Santa Clara, California.

Van Maanen, J. (1979a). Reclaiming qualitative methods for organizational research. *Administrative Science Quarterly, 24,* 520-526.

Van Maanen, J. (1979b). The fact of fiction in organizational ethnography. *Administrative Science Quarterly, 24,* 539-550.

Van Maanen, J. (1988). *Tales of the field: On writing ethnography.* Chicago: University of Chicago Press.

Van Maanen, J., & Barley, S. R. (1985). Cultural organizations: Fragments of a theory. In L. R. Pondy, P. J. Frost, G. Morgan, & T. C. Dandridge (Eds.), *Organizational symbolism.* Greenwich, CT: JAI.

Vinton, K. (1983, March). *Humor in the work-place: It's more than telling jokes.* Paper presented at the Western Academy of Management Meeting, Santa Barbara, CA.

Wacker, G. (1979). *The use of cognitive maps in a case study of the evolution of an industrial organization.* Unpublished doctoral dissertation, University of California, Los Angeles, Graduate School of Management.

Webb, E. J., Campbell, D. T., Schwartz, R. D., & Sechrest, I. (1966). *Unobtrusive measures.* Chicago: Rand McNally.

Weber, A. (1920). Prinzipielles zur Kultursoziologie [Principle issues regarding cultural sociology]. *Archiv für Sozialwissenschaft und Sozialpolitik, 47,* 1-49.

Weber, M. (1946). *The theory of social and economic organization* (A. H. Henderson, Trans.; Talcott Parsons, Ed.). New York: Oxford University Press.

Weick, K. E. (1979). *The social psychology of organizing* (2nd ed.). Reading, MA: Addison-Wesley.

Weiner, B. (1980). *Human motivation.* New York: Holt, Rinehart & Winston.

Weiss, J., & Delbecq, A. (1987). High-technology cultures and management: Silicon Valley and Route 128. *Group and Organization Studies, 12*(1), 39-54.

White, L. A. (1959). The concept of culture. *American Anthropologist, 61,* 227-251.

White, W. F. (1943). *Street-corner society: The social structure of an Italian slum.* Chicago: University of Chicago Press.

Wilkins, A. (1978). *Organizational stories as an expression of management philosophy: Implications for social control in organizations.* Unpublished doctoral dissertation, Stanford University, Graduate School of Business.

Wilkins, A., & Martin, J. (1979). *Organizational legends* (Working paper). Provo, UT/Stanford, CA: Brigham Young University and Stanford University, Graduate Schools of Business.

Index

About the Author

Sonja A. Sackmann is currently a faculty member at the University of St. Gallen and head of development in the behavioral area of the Management Zentrum St. Gallen (MZSG) in Switzerland. Previously she taught at the Graduate School of Management at the University of California, Los Angeles (UCLA), and in the Interdisciplinary Department of Business and Administration at the University of Vienna, Austria. Since 1980 she has consulted and conducted workshops and seminars both in the United States and in Europe. Her client organizations range from *Fortune* 500 to owner-managed firms. In her teaching, research, writing, and consulting, she specializes in the areas of organizational culture, personal and organizational development and change, decision making in nonroutine situations, leadership, and human resource management. Her monographs and professional papers have been published both in Europe and in the United States. She received her B.S. and M.S. in psychology from the Ruprecht-Karl University, Heidelberg, Germany. She obtained her Ph.D. in management from UCLA in 1985.

NOTES